THE ACCIDENT

"This is an adventure book! And don't believe Gerry's claim that it was all an accident. It's a tale of effort, enthusiasm and enterprise. Enjoy it."

Senator Feargal Quinn, founder of Superquinn

"Gerry Murphy's book shows vividly a restless entrepreneurial spirit in action, from the regeneration initiatives in his native Churchtown village in north Cork to the audacious establishment of the GreatGas service stations."

Senator Mary White, co-founder of Lir Chocolates

"Gerry is a fantastic businessperson. This book is both interesting and insightful, a must-read for any business owner. Gerry's passion, creativity and determination are inspiring."

Bobby Kerr, chairman of Insomnia, founding panelist on Dragon's Den and radio broadcaster

"Passion and integrity are two of Gerry's greatest qualities, qualities very evident throughout his life and this book. If you aspire to owning your own business, *The Accidental Entrepreneur* will inspire and set you on course."

John Lowe, the Money Doctor

THE ACCIDENTAL ENTREPRENEUR

How we turned €3,749 into a €100 million business in three years

Gerry Murphy

ORPEN PRESS

Published by
Orpen Press
Lonsdale House
Avoca Avenue
Blackrock
Co. Dublin
Ireland

email: info@orpenpress.com
www.orpenpress.com

Paperback ISBN 978-1-909895-59-1
ePub ISBN 978-1-909895-60-7
Kindle ISBN 978-1-909895-61-4
PDF ISBN 978-1-909895-62-1

Typeset in Minion Pro, 11 pts

Cover design concept by Keaney Design and Hayes Design.

Please note, some identities have been changed to protect the privacy of individuals and organisations.

Printed in Dublin by SPRINT-print Ltd

DEDICATION

The Accidental Entrepreneur is dedicated to my wife, Dorothy; my daughters, Niamh and Deirdre; and my late parents, Jack (1920–2000) and Nora Murphy (1923–2013).

I also dedicate this book to Ailbhe O'Reilly, commissioning editor at Orpen Press; Eileen O'Brien, my editor at Orpen Press; and most especially Jonathan Self, a friend for 28 years since we first met at the International Direct Marketing Conference in Montreaux, Switzerland in April 1986. Without Ailbhe and Eileen's interest and support and Jonathan's input, help, advice, research suggestions and encouragement, you simply would not be reading this book.

GM

About the Author

Gerry Murphy holds a Bachelor in Financial Services degree from University College Dublin and a Masters in Business Administration from Fordham University, New York, for which he studied at the Irish Management Institute. He also holds an Advanced Diploma in Public Relations from the Institute of Public Relations in Ireland. All his studies were completed as a mature student.

Gerry is a Fellow of the Institute of Bankers in Ireland, having worked in banking for 25 years with Bank of Ireland and First National Building Society before setting up the not-for-profit Churchtown Village Renewal Trust in 1997. In 2001 he was named Cork Person of the Year for his 'visionary rural renewal initiative'. In 2005 he founded GreatGas Petroleum (Ireland) plc. He holds many other non-executive director-ships and works as an international management services provider.

Gerry is a former director and chairman of the not-for-profit organisation Guaranteed Irish (a national body promoting the sale of Irish-manufactured goods and services) and former chairman of the European Union's THERMIE project for Ireland. He was also the executive producer of *Bloom*, a feature film released in 2004 based on the novel *Ulysses* by James Joyce.

The author's royalties from the sale of this book will be donated to Churchtown Historical & Heritage Society.

www.accidentalentrepreneur.me

CONTENTS

Contents

FOREWORD

The Accidental Entrepreneur is as much about the author's attention to detail as it is about becoming successful in business by accident. Equally, it demonstrates the essential characteristic needed to be successful in business, whether by accident or design, which is the unremitting sense of passion for their business activity that all self-made successful entrepreneurs have in abundance.

Gerry Murphy, time and again, underestimates himself. Not only does his book illustrate his attention to detail, he is also extremely well organised with extensive knowledge and management skills.

Gerry concludes that building a business is a creative activity and says it is one of the most exciting, interesting and all-consuming activities that one can be involved in. It is a lifetime commitment, and, although making a profit is essential, and a method by which an entrepreneur can measure their success, I agree that it isn't just about money. Money itself is only a small part of the pleasure derived from being a successful entrepreneur. Gerry sums it up when he says, 'We are in business because we love it.'

But that is not to say that there isn't a tide in the affairs of us all, in the words of Shakespeare, that, taken at the flood, leads onto fortune even by accident. Out of events and circumstances which no one could predict or indeed control, arise opportunities that a potential accidental entrepreneur will be the first to recognise and take advantage of.

Sir David Barclay KSG

INTRODUCTION

At 5.30 p.m. on Friday 22 April 2005, while I was filling my car with petrol, I bumped into a business contact called Seán Lewis. During our brief conversation, I mentioned an issue that happened to be irritating me. Seán's response was a casual comment, the sort of reply one makes when one is in the middle of doing something else, but what he said gave me the germ of an idea for a new business.

Although the idea immediately resonated, it seemed an act of folly to take it any further. I had no real experience of the industry concerned, I was working almost full time on a not-for-profit project that was very important to me and, anyway, I didn't have any spare capital.

And yet, having had the idea, I simply couldn't put it out of my mind. I thought about it on the drive home, as I lay in bed that night and when I awoke the following morning. In fact, I spent that Saturday writing up a very rough business plan and worked out a way whereby, for a relatively small outlay, I could quickly discover whether the idea had legs.

I think it is fair to say that it did have legs. Three years after it was launched the business was turning over €100 million and was profitable. Not a bad result, considering that my initial investment was €3,749 and I only ever worked for the company on a part-time basis.

The purpose of this book is not, however, to show off my entrepreneurial skills. Far from it. As you will soon find out, the venture was a complete accident, it came close to collapsing on several occasions and its eventual success was dependent less on me than on the company's full-time management. Moreover, my business career has been littered with enough failures to instil in me a proper sense of modesty.

No, I am writing this book in the hope that it will encourage others to take the plunge and follow their entrepreneurial dreams. If it inspires just one person to start his or her own business, I will be satisfied. It might also be useful to pass on some of the practical things I have learned (often at considerable emotional and financial expense) since I gave up a secure, well-paid job and pursued my own interests.

I use the word 'interests' because although I have enjoyed launching and managing a number of what are referred to as 'small to medium-sized enterprises', I have by no means confined myself to commerce. Indeed, any business successes I have had can all, without exception, be traced back to wholly non-commercial activities. The main business described in this book, for example, came from my desire to regenerate the village where I was born.

I don't want to give the impression that I am wholly uninterested in money. I enjoy the security and privileges that it brings. It is, however, incidental rather than an end in itself. What excites me is creating something from nothing, solving problems and improving other people's lives.

I have noticed that businesspeople who are primarily driven by profit frequently come unstuck, often sooner rather than later. I don't place much importance on having a good idea, either. This may strike you as odd, given that I am making such a fuss about the concept that allowed me to build up a €100 million company in three years, but most business ideas are both simple and unoriginal. Success in business is largely about execution. Execution is a skill that can be acquired and, for this reason, I am firmly of the belief that anyone who wants to can become an entrepreneur.

I started working for myself relatively late in life. Until I was 43, I had only had two employers: a bank and a building society. Neither of these organisations really encouraged creativity, experimentation or (ironically, when one looks at what has happened in the financial services sector) risk-taking. I was set up for a quiet, conservative life working for 'the man' until I retired and then a quiet, conservative life until I died. But a series of unconnected, random events changed the way I thought about things and – well – the way I behaved. I ended up breaking free from corporate life and going into business. No one could have been more surprised than me. I am, in short, an entirely accidental entrepreneur.

I first started 'writing a book' in August 1997 on a family holiday in Malta. At the swimming pool I managed to write almost 20,000 words on a little Psion Organiser and this text was eventually published in *The Annals of Churchtown* in 2005. That publication and the stories of the early influences on my life inspired *The Accidental Entrepreneur*. I hope you enjoy my story.

GM

PART I

THE GREATGAS STORY

How I Became an Accidental Entrepreneur

The story of how we turned a €3,749 investment into a €100 million business in just three years can be traced back to two wholly unconnected events, the first of which occurred as long ago as 1995.

That year was the hottest Irish summer on record. Where I live, in south County Dublin, I only remember it raining twice in seven weeks, and that was at night. The temperature hovered in the high 20s and even broke the 30-degree barrier on several occasions.

In a country more famous for its rainfall, the effect of day after day of sun cannot be understated. People were in a cheerful, ebullient mood. Sales of garden furniture, barbecues, Bermuda shorts, Hawaiian shirts, ice cream and suntan lotion shot through the roof. Those who had paid for an overseas holiday bemoaned their bad luck and frequently returned disappointed because the weather abroad hadn't been as good as the weather at home. There was an outbreak of al fresco dining, cafés and pubs moved their wooden tables and chairs onto the pavements, and one no longer needed to be a masochist to venture a dip in the sea.

There was another reason for this national sense of optimism. Ever since the end of the 1980s, the Irish economy had been growing. Indeed, 1995 is generally considered the first year of the Celtic Tiger. Inflation was down, gross domestic product was up and our trade deficits had been transformed into annual surpluses. Moreover, we were attracting serious foreign investment – barely a week seemed to pass without some huge multinational announcing plans to relocate part of its business to Ireland. Things were so buoyant that those who had emigrated in tougher times to find work were now coming home. The Northern Ireland peace process was well advanced. In short, after hundreds of years of depression, repression and oppression, the country was finally coming into its own. Anything, we all felt, was possible.

It was against this background that the first event took place. Actually, it wasn't an event per se, more the anticipation of an event. In 1995 I was 41 years old and the group operations director of First National Building Society. By profession I was a banker. Nowadays bankers are reviled, but at that time our greatest collective sin was the size of our account charges, and the strongest emotion we evoked was one of mild disdain. Although my career had not been without its moments of interest, it could hardly be described as exciting. I joined Bank of Ireland at the age of eighteen and worked my way up from the lowliest of positions in a tiny rural branch to become the Dublin-based senior manager in charge of advertising. In 1989 I left Bank of Ireland and joined First National as an assistant general manager, and in 1994 I was appointed to its board as an executive director.

In a way, it is surprising that I achieved any sort of success as a banker. Financial institutions are conservative by nature and, although not exactly resistant to change, they tend to move slowly. I would hardly describe myself as a firecracker, but I am quick to make up my mind and never hesitate when it comes to taking action. It is in my nature to continually challenge the status quo. It is ironic, therefore, that it was my fellow directors' decision to challenge the status quo that was to help set me on such a very different course.

In 1995 First National, which had been founded in 1861 as the Workingman's Benefit Building Society, was the longest established building society in Ireland. It was a 'mutual' – that is, owned by its members. To become a member you merely had to open an appropriate savings account. The previous year we had seen one of our closest competitors, the Irish Permanent Building Society, demutualise and become a public company. During the process, its members each received shares worth £540, the right to purchase more shares at a favourable price and the guarantee of free bonus shares in the future. The directors and senior management had also received substantial share allocations.

When, early in 1995, one of my fellow directors suggested that First National should also demutualise, I was not wholly against it. The Society's mutual status was making it difficult for us to raise funds and thus expand. Nor could I overlook the fact that demutualisation would, by my standards, probably make me a wealthy man. I calculated that, if it went ahead, by the age of 50 I would never have to work again. When, like me, you come from a relatively modest, middle-class farming background, the thought of getting your hands on a substantial sum of money can colour your judgement. I convinced myself that demutualisation would be best for the Society, but if I am honest I kept thinking about what it would really mean for me.

I found it rather inconvenient, therefore, when my conscience started to play up. This isn't the place to debate the arguments for and against demutualisation; suffice to say that I concluded it would be wrong to support it. I couldn't see how it was in the interests of our customers or how it would lead to a stronger, more competitive institution. I also felt that it went against the ethos of the organisation, which had been established by and for its members, and I also suspected that First National wasn't lean or mean enough to survive as a public company. Moreover, the entire scheme would primarily benefit a handful of directors (not least myself) and staff, while simultaneously destroying 144 years of tradition. Towards the end of 1995, it became clear that nothing would stop the demutualisation of First National. I knew that I was going to have to decide how to respond.

I did not have to decide how to respond to the second event; I was flabbergasted by it. The newspaper headline on the front page of the *Evening Echo* on Saturday 18 January 1997 – 'This pub has been moved to Vienna ...' – may not sound particularly dramatic, but I was intimately acquainted with the pub in question. Flannery's had been the main bar in my home place. To read that its fixtures and fittings had been sold, lock, stock and, as it were, barrels, to a company specialising in creating Irish-themed pubs abroad, and that it had been reassembled in Vienna, was something of a shock.

I am not sure that anyone knows exactly when Flannery's was first opened, but it was certainly trading in the 1850s. The fittings were late Victorian and had been designed to accommodate both a bar and a shop on the same premises. This custom of combining a bar with a retail establishment, referred to as 'spirit groceries', is peculiarly Irish and came about in the mid-nineteenth century when the temperance movement forced publicans to diversify in order to make up for falling alcohol sales. At any rate, Flannery's had a long history and was owned at one point by the forefathers of the author Maeve Binchy.

Its disappearance saddened me, but not for sentimental reasons or because I am much of a drinker. Flannery's – and a thousand bars like it up and down the country – was much more than a place to seek refreshment, eat or buy groceries. It was where people went to meet, talk and exchange news. It is no exaggeration to describe these pubs as the heart of any village. It was potentially the death knell of the community when Flannery's was closed, ripped out and taken overseas. It is not as if other village facilities such as churches, sub-post offices and shops were faring any better. For me, the loss of Flannery's was really about the end of Irish rural life, as generation upon generation had known it, and as I had known it.

No clear plan came to me as I read the article about Flannery's. I didn't make any resolutions or decide upon any particular course of action. Rather, it set me thinking. I realised that, although I regularly went home to visit my family, I had cut myself off from my past. I admitted to myself just how much I missed my roots and, in particular, the things that make Irish rural life special: authenticity, community and productivity. I also found myself yearning for the rich, flat countryside of my native north County Cork and for the friends with whom I had lost touch. More than anything else, I regretted the fact that Churchtown was slowly dying. Could anything be done, I asked myself, to restore its fortunes and give it a meaningful future?

The impending demutualisation of First National and the sale of Flannery's both occupied a good deal of my thoughts during the spring and early summer of 1997. My business and personal life carried on as normal, but nothing could shake the feeling that I was going to have to make some major changes in my life. I had to do something.

Since the early 1990s, I had been trying to buy a little house in Churchtown, but every time I came close to agreeing a deal my father would raise an objection. Sometimes this was based on the cost:

Me: I'm buying the derelict house next to O'Sullivan's.
Father: What are you paying for it?
Me: Five thousand.
Father: Five thousand? It isn't worth two!

On other occasions there were more complex forces at work:

Me: I'm buying Pat's late mother's place, so don't tell me I'm paying too much.
Father: What are they looking for?
Me: Four thousand.
Father: That's not so bad.
Me: I'm glad you approve.
Father: But there's no way you can buy it. His cousin Joe has been waiting seven years to buy that house.

Finally, in 1997, while I was wrestling with the question of my future, I managed to buy up a major portion of the village in secret. 'A major portion of the village' has a rather impressive ring to it, but what I actually purchased was the Market House and its neighbours, a group of cut-stone Georgian buildings located in *centre-ville* Churchtown, including what had been Flannery's. One of the larger buildings was derelict and had a tree growing on the roof, an ash if I remember correctly, and the rest of the property was not in much better condition.

Laurence J. Peter, famous for *The Peter Principle*, in which he points out that every employee tends to rise to the level of his incompetence, once said: 'If you don't know where you are going, you will probably end up somewhere else.' There's a similar Chinese proverb, 'If you don't know where you are going, any road will take you.' Both are good reminders of the importance of setting goals. Still, there are occasions when a little wandering in the desert is not a bad thing. It stimulates creativity and opens one up to the possibilities of chance.

In August 1997, the same month that I completed the purchase of the Market House and Flannery's, I resigned from First National. The building society had, in a manner of speaking, been pushing me away, whereas Churchtown had been pulling me closer. I had lots of vague thoughts about what I would do next but only one concrete plan. It occurred to me that, as my new property was far too large to be a single dwelling house, I would turn it into some sort of a business. Thus, by a slow and circuitous route, I ceased to be an employee and, without intending to, became an entrepreneur.

2

CORNERING THE BALLYBUNION LETTUCE MARKET

My family have farmed the same land on the edge of Churchtown for many generations, but early on I knew it was not for me. It was a tough life and in the 1960s and 1970s farm incomes had fallen. There was enough money to send me away to boarding school, but university would have been a stretch. I could probably have stayed on the farm and helped my father had I wished, but at eighteen I was full of the spirit of adventure. I wanted to make my own way in the world.

In 1972 the options for a school leaver in north Cork were limited. There was a serious scarcity of work, and jobs that offered any sort of career potential were few and far between. It was, after all, still a largely agricultural economy without much industry. My choices were to emigrate or to try to get into one of the few sectors that promised the prospect of promotion, such as the civil service, insurance or banking. Today there is a great emphasis on personal fulfilment and young people are encouraged to select an occupation that interests them, but when I was offered a position at Bank of Ireland I didn't think to question what I would be doing, or whether I would enjoy it. I took the job and was grateful for a chance to prove myself.

I started as an assistant. My main task was to take the customer's savings book and write in the details of each transaction after the cashier had dealt with it. At this level, advancement in the bank was largely linked to length of service and, to a lesser extent, passing a series of banking exams. Many of my colleagues did these at a decidedly leisurely pace, sometimes allowing years to pass before sitting the next paper, but I tackled them all in a matter of eighteen months. I was ambitious. If you wanted to progress upwards through the bank, the route was more or less prescribed. The moment I achieved one objective, I set my sights on the next. When I became a senior bank official I was already thinking about how to become an assistant manager, and after that a manager, and after that ... you get the picture. In corporate life, the next rung of the ladder and all the rungs above it are clearly visible all the way to the top, which is where I intended to be.

I don't think it would be an understatement to say that I was driven. My motivation was not money; I was pushing myself, and pushing myself hard, for entirely different reasons. I take enormous pleasure in solving problems and every new role brought with it a satisfying volume of obstacles and challenges for me to deal with. I also believed (incorrectly as it turned out) that the higher I reached the more liberty and autonomy I would enjoy.

It isn't easy to sum up the quarter of a century I spent in banking. I have already expressed surprise that I managed to do as well as I did. This isn't false modesty on my part, but because I am impatient, insistent and impetuous and these are not seen as good personality traits in a banker. Or, come to think of it, in anyone else. Of course, it is true that I specialised in marketing, where there is a greater degree of tolerance, but even there I was often in conflict with my superiors, and I am sure that they frequently viewed me as a dreadful nuisance, regardless of anything I managed to achieve.

And what did I achieve? At the time I thought it was rather a lot. I could list multiple projects that seemed valuable and important while I was undertaking them. But what does it really matter if, in 1984, I managed to cut Bank of Ireland's print bill by a substantial sum of money? Or if, in 1992, I helped to increase First National's share of the mortgage market by 18 per cent? The fact is that my greatest achievements during those 25 years were all personal. I went to university (at my employer's expense), learned innumerable skills, made all sorts of mistakes (for which I didn't have to pay), tested myself (and, I'm afraid, others) and earned a good income. In the period immediately after I left banking I was sometimes inclined to be critical of my employers and even more critical of myself. Banking had stifled me and I had allowed it to. Gradually, however, I came to the realisation that I had come away from banking a far richer person (both figuratively and literally), and that I was wrong to complain.

Sometimes, when people give up something they have been doing all their lives – whether it is a particular job or raising children or playing a sport – they can feel at a loss. The sudden freedom throws them, and it takes time to adjust to their new life. I suffered no such experience on walking away from First National. I was ecstatic. At the age of 43 I felt like I had my life back. I was free for the first time. I woke up every morning in a state bordering on euphoria.

One of the main reasons why many employees don't give up their job and become self-employed is that they are worried about the risk. I *was* concerned before I took the plunge. My assessment of the risk, however, was poor. I thought, for instance, that I was giving up a safe job, but in reality there's no such thing as secure employment. Even the most senior personnel are in constant danger of being made redundant and after a certain age it is by no means certain that one will find another, equivalent position. I also believed that being an entrepreneur meant taking on financial risk. So it can, but it depends entirely on how you organise your business affairs. I also imagined the shame of failure, but I see now that to stay on in a job that didn't fulfil me would have been a greater shame and a greater failure. Anyway, failure turns out to be both educational and stimulating, and, as will become clear presently, I should know. Finally, if you don't follow your dreams you risk feeling a deep sense of regret and disappointment. Horace wrote something that sums this up nicely: 'Seize the day! Rejoice while you are alive; enjoy the day; live life to the fullest; make the most of what you have. It is later than you think.'

Having completed an MBA in 1990, my intention, when I resigned, was to work on a doctorate. I had enrolled at Trinity College Dublin six months previously and had planned to work on my thesis when and as my other duties allowed. Now I was free to pursue my studies full time. My subject was corporate governance and it was at the back of my mind to become a professional non-executive director. I envisaged half-a-dozen lucrative appointments to public company boards, where my only work would be to spend the odd hour in my leather-book-lined study making highly pertinent notes on reports with a gold propelling pencil (the fact that I had neither a leather-book-lined study nor a gold propelling pencil was no barrier to this fantasy) and attend monthly board meetings.

I loved the rarefied, academic atmosphere of Trinity. It was a privilege to be a student at a college that counted Jonathan Swift, Edmund Burke, Oscar Wilde, Samuel Beckett, Douglas Hyde and innumerable other luminaries among its former students. I was much enamoured of the academic life, by the other doctoral students and by my professors. Indeed, I can honestly say that for the whole time I was at Trinity I was never happier.

Never happier, but also never more bored. Corporate governance, I quickly realised, was not a subject I should be tangling with. What I wanted was to be up and doing, not pouring my energy into deciphering the mysteries of complex EU legislation. One day, about six weeks into the second year, I said to myself, 'It's kaput for corporate governance!' and went to look for a more interesting occupation.

What I soon found was that I had a passion for starting (and growing) small to medium-sized businesses. Having always assumed that I was, in essence, a corporate animal, this discovery took me by surprise. But not my late mother, who said she had suspected as much ever since I had attempted to corner the Ballybunion lettuce market.

When I was young my family used to go to the Kerry seaside resort of Ballybunion every summer for our holidays. In 1965, aged eleven, I decided that this holiday would be all the more pleasurable with some extra pocket money. What the area lacked, it seemed to me, was a supply of fresh lettuce. I worked out the optimum time to plant and spent several tense weeks worrying about whether my crop would be ready for cutting on the right day. It was, and with considerable difficulty I managed to find space in the family car (barely large enough to accommodate the six of us and our luggage) for my produce. I recall harsh words being spoken by my siblings when asked, with perfect politeness, to carry boxes of lettuce on their laps for the two hours it would take to make the journey. They made the sacrifice in vain for, try as I might, I couldn't persuade any shop in Ballybunion to buy my lettuces. Like so many businesspeople before me, I had failed to consider the distribution and sales part of the equation. One doesn't need a degree in psychology to suspect that this oversight may have been the cause of my subsequent interest in marketing.

My interest in marketing turned out to be an invaluable asset when I was searching for business opportunities. It enabled me to see how new ideas could be made to work and to turn around unsuccessful enterprises. Within months of leaving First National I was examining all sorts of possibilities, from a medical clinic to a football-themed café, from a radio station to a management consultancy. None of these ventures, however, excited me as much as the first business project (salad excepted) that I ever took on.

3

CONFESSIONS OF A SECRET SIGNPOST FITTER

'Gerry Murphy has bought the Market House.'
'Who?'
'Jack's son.'
'What's he done?'
'He's bought the Market House. Oh, and Flannery's.'
'What on earth would he want to go and do that for?'
'I haven't the faintest clue.'

I think it is fair to say that this snippet of overheard conversation pretty much sums up Churchtown opinion about my acquisition. The bemusement was understandable. The population of the village had been falling steadily since the 1940s. It took an especially bad knock in 1951 when Vincent O'Brien, the world-famous horse trainer, moved his establishment to Tipperary, and another in 1982, when the creamery finally closed. By 1997 a third of the village houses were empty and in considerable disrepair. All that was left in the village was a small shop, a sub-post office and O'Brien's pub, with Flannery's – or O'Sullivan's as it had become by then – having closed in 1992. Two bars generally do better than one in Irish villages. This is because if someone goes into one bar and sees a person they don't get on with they have somewhere else to go, whereas if there isn't a choice they will drink at home or journey further afield.

I had left Churchtown in 1972 because of the lack of opportunity, and many of my generation followed suit. From 1972 to 1997 little had changed and, of course, the population was not just declining, it was ageing too. Indeed, the only significant venture in the village for decades had been a nursing home developed by the Fehan family in 1995. The Celtic Tiger may have been starting to roar all over the rest of the country, but it only just mewed in Churchtown.

What made Churchtown's decline all the more poignant was its singular beauty. It is located three miles from the nearest main road in lush, lightly wooded and extremely peaceful countryside. The land is flat and a slow-moving river, the Awbeg, snakes its way along the northern edge of the parish. The whole area is crisscrossed with streams, and boreens meander among the patchwork of fields. The village itself contains several fine Georgian (or as near to Georgian as makes no difference) stone-cut buildings, a thirteenth-century graveyard and a ruined church. In short, it is as idyllic a spot as you could wish for.

People may have wondered what I wanted with several large, near-derelict buildings in a tiny, off-the-map village which no one had heard of and no one ever went to. So did I. My original intention had been to buy a small, manageable house that my family and I could use for weekends and holidays. I was conscious that neither of my daughters had much knowledge of where they came from. They knew their grandparents and uncles, of course, but their bond with Churchtown wasn't as strong as I would have liked. My daughters had been raised in Dublin. They had no experience of village life or rural Ireland. They were the youngest members of a family who had lived and farmed in the same area for hundreds of years and yet, in the space of a single generation, they had become so completely removed from it that Churchtown may as well have been in a foreign country.

Had I a dozen daughters, once the buildings I had bought were restored I could have accommodated them all with room to spare, and it was this that gave me the idea for how to use the space. On the principle of 'build it and they will come', I decided to create a holiday hostel, conference centre, restaurant and bar. The restoration work itself was a pleasure, in no small part because I worked with a builder I really liked. In fact, Maurice Gilbert and I liked each other so much that we became business partners.

Many entrepreneurs feel that their interests are best served by holding on to as high a percentage of shares as possible. If the reason you are in business is to make money and only to make money, this is probably correct. For me, developing a business is a creative process and the most satisfying aspect of it is finding a way to meet the varied needs of customers, staff, suppliers and shareholders. I would never become involved in a business that didn't bring tangible benefits to everyone involved. I am certainly not holding myself out as a paragon of virtue or someone who is especially ethical; I am driven, like any entrepreneur, by profit. However, in my experience, if a concept works there is plenty of return for everyone, and if it flops the size of one's stake is completely irrelevant.

I called my new venture Boss Murphy's, after my great-grandfather, William Murphy, who was born in 1831 and died in 1911. William was a farmer, historian, raconteur, musician and instrument maker, well known in the local area for his fiddle playing. He was a tenant farmer until the 1885 Ashbourne Act gave him the right to buy his land from his British landlord on terms that today seem harsh – a 49-year mortgage at 4 per cent interest a year. It was probably after he bought our family farm that he acquired the sobriquet 'Boss'. He travelled a good deal, twice making the arduous journey to Iowa, USA to visit two sons and a daughter who had emigrated there. Boss Murphy was an enterprising man and seemed to me an entirely appropriate ancestor after whom to name my hospitality business.

I am confident, for I believe he had a lively sense of humour, that the Boss would have enjoyed my own enterprise in planning the new business. However, it soon occurred to me that, given how off the beaten track the village is, no one would be able to find Boss Murphy's or, for that matter, Churchtown itself. The area suffers badly from that all too familiar rural complaint: narrow, screened lanes that set firmly off in one direction and then abruptly turn back on themselves before heading off somewhere completely different. On a foggy, pre-satnav day you could circle Churchtown for quite a while and never find it, no matter how you twisted and turned. Knowing that the county council would take forever to fund the cost of adequate signposting on the surrounding roads, I decided to erect my own. I am not quite sure what the penalty is for forging official signage and installing it in a prominent position without appropriate planning permission, but I deserve to be punished. In the middle of the day, with the help of a person or persons unknown (I fully intend to protect the guilty), I put the signs up and since then, to my intense pleasure, the council has numbered each sign and added them to its asset register.

I was as prepared for Boss Murphy's to fail as I was for it to thrive. As it happened, it hovered somewhere between the two extremes. What I hadn't anticipated was the effect that the relatively insignificant achievement of establishing a small business in the place where I was born would have on my psyche. It filled me with optimism and energy. What had been undertaken as a gentle experiment to see if I could improve my home place had roused and inspired me. Even in the first stages of getting Boss Murphy's off the ground, I realised that what would give me the greatest satisfaction in life would be to try to reverse the village's decline, expand the community and ensure its sustainability. This was an ambitious objective but a worthwhile one. It would give me the excuse I wanted to spend more time there, and it might be fun (after a quarter of a century in banking, fun was high on my agenda). I could see that there were others in the neighbourhood who felt the same way. If I could help renew the village, it would be some sort of legacy. What I am trying to explain is that the last thing on my mind was the idea of building up a €100 million company.

4

The Fundamental Interconnectedness of All Things

I know from dark hints and veiled comments (and because they also said it outright) that there are two schools of thought among my nearest and dearest regarding what happened after I decided to devote myself to the renewal of Churchtown. School A believes I overdid it and that while I was in the grip of a sort of entrepreneurial fever I took on more than was sensible. Its members don't exactly claim that things got out of hand or accuse me of being obsessive, but this is probably only because they are too polite. While the process was going on, the members of School A generally responded to news of my growing number of initiatives with a roll of their eyes and a 'Well, you know what Gerry is like.' School B is more sympathetic. Its members believe that I had finally found something I enjoyed doing. Far from being obsessive, I was simply throwing myself into it. They point out that I was on a bit of a roll and, naturally, wanted to take full advantage of it. True, they admit, some of my projects came to nought, but what of it?

Both schools were right and, either way, there is no denying the fact that once I had committed myself to Churchtown I was wholly absorbed by the task. I can't pretend that it was all perfectly thought out, because it wasn't. One thing led to another and that led to something else ... and so on. I was constantly inventing and experimenting. It wasn't completely unstructured, however. I had a purpose and a vision. If Churchtown was to have a future, it needed employment, housing and services. If new people were to be attracted to the area they had to know about the village and what advantages it offered.

Happily, I was not working alone. There were many others in Churchtown and its environs who felt as I did, not least the members of the Churchtown Development Association. However, I felt there was room for a second organisation and founded a village trust. The new Churchtown Village Renewal Trust began life with a seven-year regeneration plan and sixteen specific objectives. These ranged from publishing a history of the parish to restoring its public and private buildings and from improving the sports facilities to encouraging an entrepreneurial environment. When the seven years were up in 2004, all but five of the objectives had been achieved and some of these, with the benefit of hindsight, were a little unrealistic. For instance, I seem to recall insisting that the village would support 'the creation of a pan-European teleworking initiative', and I can't even remember now what I meant by it. So, if one strikes off the more nebulous aspirations from the list, the Trust delivered on its promises.

The sort of projects undertaken included (but were by no means confined to) restoring and extending the community centre, restoring various other buildings in the village, commissioning public art, developing a network of walking trails, publishing *The Annals of Churchtown* (a local history blockbuster running to 766 pages) and helping to fundraise for a new GAA sports centre. The Trust also marketed Churchtown to a wider audience with merchandising, signage and publicity. Any one of these projects deserves a book to itself. For example, as part of the public art programme the village now has several pieces of monumental sculpture. Or, to cite another example, the GAA members raised several hundred thousand euros over two years by raffling a house.

I contributed where I could and set out to revive the village in other ways. My first move was to become a somewhat diffident property developer. Diffident because, although I enjoyed the design process and construction challenges, my primary aim was to attract new residents rather than to make a profit. This is lucky because my tendency to over-specify and under-price everything meant that I never made much money out of development. Indeed, the whole thing would have been a disaster but for a stroke of good luck. I had acquired more land than I could afford to build on, and was able to cover my costs and make a surplus by selling the land on to others.

My priority, after I had bought the Market House and Flannery's, was to establish a base in Churchtown, and I did this by immediately renovating sufficient space for an apartment and office suite. Once completed, I used this as the headquarters for my business activities, wherever they were located. As I have explained, once I gave up my doctorate I was exceptionally busy looking at possible start-ups and acquisitions. As with the Churchtown Village Renewal Trust, I was working more on instinct than to a specific plan. My thought was to use my savings, marketing skills and contacts to find and develop a portfolio of businesses.

What one learns, after devoting time and money to a number of unproven businesses, is that a distressingly high percentage of them do not prosper. I have already admitted to my lack of success as a property developer, but there are some other disasters from this period that I would like to get off my chest. The most public of these, without a doubt, was the Red Café. I chaired a team of investors who, after a long negotiation, won the right to open a chain of Manchester United-themed cafés throughout Britain and Ireland. The first of these was in the centre of Dublin. On paper it should have been a triumph: Manchester United was one of the world's most famous sports brands, we had experienced catering partners, there was a star-studded launch and the café was in a central location. It certainly attracted a great deal of publicity, but to no avail, for it never attracted enough customers to make it viable.

Another venture that did not attract enough customers to make it viable was Boss Murphy's, Dortmund. Following on from Boss Murphy's, Churchtown, I nurtured high but unfulfilled hopes of launching an international chain of Irish pubs. My hopes for George's Street Technology, an online share-dealing business, and My Tradesman, a sales portal for home repairs and decoration, were also unfulfilled. I did no better with the Kendlebell franchise I bought (Kendlebell being a virtual office service). I lost quite a bit of money, too, investing in a film production of James Joyce's *Ulysses*. Entitled *Bloom* and featuring an accomplished cast led by Stephen Rea, Angeline Ball and Hugh O'Conor, the film suffered from the Ballybunion Lettuce Problem: lack of distribution.

I didn't mind losing money on *Bloom* because I felt that the film and its director, Sean Walsh, were worth supporting. I felt the same way about the Churchtown village shop, which I bought when the proprietors decided to retire. I tried advertising it, moving it to larger premises and investing in more stock, but although sales kept growing profit remained elusive.

The astute reader will have noticed that I am reconciled to all the losses I have listed. This isn't any kind of bravado on my part. Poverty and business failure don't frighten me, because they can't affect the things I treasure most in life, namely my wife, our children, our family's continued good health and the freedom to do what I love doing. The only aspect of closing a business down that ever distresses me is if there are employees involved. On the occasions when this has happened I have tried my best – which sometimes has not been enough – to make sure everyone is looked after properly. If a business fails, my concern is to work out why (that way I am in a better position to avoid making the same mistakes next time round) and to move on. Afterwards, I attempt to work harder, more carefully and with greater ingenuity.

It is quite tempting to pretend that I experienced failure after failure, came close to giving up and then, finally, when I was in total despair, achieved one good, solid success. This would make a much more dramatic and moral tale. What actually happened was that I had enough successes to pay for the Churchtown renewal projects I had chosen to sponsor, cover my business blunders and invest in new ventures. This has a nice, tidy ring to it, the gains paying for the losses and a bit more besides, but the reality was a bit messier and my cash flow was sometimes more of a cash dribble and even, on occasion, a cash drought.

The companies that did well have no more in common with each other than the companies that did poorly. The Sims Clinic did very well. Its two partners, Doctors Tony Walsh and David Walsh, had been about to sign a franchise agreement with a well-known London hospital when we were introduced. I can take no credit for their medical brilliance, which is the reason why Sims is now one of the leading fertility clinics in the British Isles, but I did encourage them to launch on their own and helped them financially to set up a state-of-the-art facility. I also had a small role in helping Sherry FitzGerald, the property advisory firm, to expand into a national franchise chain, and helped fund LiteFM (now Q102) to launch its radio franchise. Marble & Granite also did well and hopefully will survive the economic crash, which in itself is a fantastic achievement. Ballyhoura Apple Farm was always more of a long-term project, which is only now starting (if you will excuse me this once) to bear fruit. Speaking of Churchtown businesses that succeeded, I sold my interest in Boss Murphy's once it was up and running.

I have tried to paint a picture of my career up to the point when I launched the business that is the main subject of this book, although there are quite a few ventures that I have left out because they never amounted to much one way or the other. The switch from employee to entrepreneur occurred in 1997 and most of what I have described, especially in this chapter, took place between then and 2005. One of the interesting things I noticed during this whole period was what Dirk Gently, Douglas Adams' fictional detective, describes as 'the fundamental interconnectedness of all things'. I am not sure if it is a result of synchronicity or serendipity but people, events, decisions, places and objects that seemed to have nothing to do with each other would later turn out to be linked in unusual and unexpected ways.

5

STRIKING OIL

Like oil lamps we put them out the back —
of our houses, of our minds
… and then
a time came, this time and now
we need them.

When I first heard the opening lines of Eavan Boland's *The Emigrant Irish*, made famous by President Mary Robinson when she quoted them in a speech to the Oireachtas (Irish houses of parliament) in 1995, I was struck particularly by the words 'now we need them'. For in my own little corner of Ireland, Churchtown, one hundred and fifty years of emigration to urban areas and abroad had decimated the local population. We were committed to reinvigorating our community, but there were so few of us that the task seemed nigh on impossible. What we needed was *them* – returning emigrants and new residents. The problem was that the village had almost nothing to offer apart from a sleepy, old-world charm. Work was being done to improve the available services, but there was no disputing the lack of jobs and accommodation. It seemed to me that a Keynesian approach was called for. The local economy needed a stimulus package.

A few years later no one would have raised an eyebrow, but in 1997 the idea of building new houses and creating a village green in the depths of the north Cork countryside was greeted with bemusement.

So unexpected was my planning application to enlarge and extend the village that permission was granted in a remarkably short time. The planners expressed their doubts as to the viability of the scheme (possibly because they never believed it would proceed) but happily supported it. Many locals said we would not sell a single house.

I turned out to be the most amateur of property developers. My primary error was to over-specify. I commissioned each house as if I intended to live in it myself, specifying lots of architectural detail, room for expansion and high-quality materials. When I should have been trying to drive costs down, I couldn't stop myself pushing them up. As a result, when it came to selling the houses – and in the end we built a total of 35 – we barely broke even. When the economy improved, a more commercially minded developer took the unfinished part of the development off my hands. As has so often happened in my life, I ended up making a profit not by design but by accident.

By 2002 Churchtown was beginning to come alive again. There were now two bars, a restaurant, a hostel with conference facilities, an improved sports ground and a refurbished community centre, as well as the original post office. In this same year, Jack and Peggy O'Flaherty, the proprietors of the small general store, conscious that if they didn't expand there was a real risk another shop would open in the village and destroy their business, moved to larger premises; larger, but, not large enough. What the village was crying out for, now its population had increased, was a small supermarket.

Shortly after moving into their new premises the O'Flaherty's decided to sell. And I decided to buy. I was much taken with the idea of creating a bigger village shop. I didn't exactly imagine myself wearing an apron and standing behind the counter overseeing operations, but the thought of providing such an invaluable resource to Churchtown strongly appealed to me. I also knew that a well-stocked, well-run shop would be an effective way of attracting both inward investment and prospective inhabitants. With this in mind I started to plan purpose-built premises, although it took me a couple of years to focus on the project and another couple of years before it was finished. In the meantime, I restrained my yearnings to slice ham, weigh produce and stock shelves and instead employed a manager. It transpired there simply wasn't enough work for him to do and as a result his salary made the difference between profit and loss. It occurred to me that if I owned another second business close by, he could manage both of them.

I briefly mentioned the River Awbeg in an earlier chapter. One of its sources is in the Ballyhoura Mountains and by the time it reaches the gently rolling plane surrounding Churchtown it meanders and doubles back on itself in a manner that is quite confusing, in part because there is more than one branch. However, and this is the key point, it does connect Churchtown with another small village, Ballyhea, some five miles away. And the thing about Ballyhea is that it is home to the only petrol station on the twenty-mile stretch of the N20 road between Mallow and Charleville. Just as I was casting around for an additional local retail business to buy, this petrol station came on the market. It seemed serendipitous, so I acquired it in partnership with Maurice Gilbert and Michelle Gleeson, turned it over to our manager and congratulated myself on solving a tricky problem. Churchtown's shop, so vital to its long-term future, was secure.

On the day we closed the deal with Donie Hennessy on the Ballyhea petrol station, what I knew about the petroleum sector could have been written on the back of a till receipt. I viewed it as a single vertical business with oil wells at one end and petrol pumps at the other. Like many consumers I had an indifferent opinion of the oil companies. I wondered about the frequency with which they altered the price of fuel and felt that their gradual move into the grocery sector was damaging to small shop owners. Had the Ballyhea petrol station been profitable I am not sure that I would ever have bothered to investigate further. Within a few months, though, it was clear that the petrol station and its shop were not achieving sufficient turnover to cover costs. Reluctantly, because I was engaged with other, larger businesses, I found it prudent to become more actively involved.

The station was tied to the Estate Oil group. Estate, one of the smaller players in the Irish retail fuel market, had paid for installing the pumps and signage seven years before we purchased the business and had also made a contribution towards the cost of refurbishing the shop. In exchange they had obtained a ten-year fuel supply contract, on which three years were left to run. The downside for me was that this contract allowed them to supply fuel at pretty much whatever price they wanted. The formula fuel suppliers used to work out prices was not transparent and, I always suspected, was designed to confuse their wholesale customers. There were days, for instance, when we were forced to buy a tanker of fuel for Ballyhea for a higher price per litre than other local forecourts were selling it. Indeed, the margins on petrol and diesel were so slim that I began to understand why, especially for tied operators such as ourselves, grocery and general retail sales were so important. We tried all sorts of different strategies in the hope of generating even a modest profit. We even resorted to the very thing that had so irritated me as a consumer – regularly altering the price of fuel. I quickly found that I was on the horns of a dilemma. Higher fuel prices resulted in lower turnover both at the pump and in the shop. So, although we were making our margin, we weren't covering our overheads. Lower fuel prices resulted in dramatically increased turnover, both at the pump and in the shop. However, losses on the fuel, the need for extra staff and the extra wear and tear on the equipment meant that we still weren't covering the overheads.

One of my main frustrations was that our fuel supplier wouldn't tell us in advance what we would be paying for each tanker of fuel. It transpired that higher turnover, which we assume was good news for Estate, was bad news for us. Naturally, we raised this with them and from the end of 2004 until early 2005 we had what was, essentially, the same conversation. I would say: 'We've pushed our fuel sales from ten thousand to fifty thousand litres a week, but we're making nothing. We've become busy fools. We need a better margin.' They would say: 'Well, we gave the business you bought a grant in 1996 to set up the filling station. We expect to make a return on our money. We will give you a slightly better price, but don't expect anything else.'

At that juncture we could have done what many forecourt owners in a similar position were doing: secretly buy fuel from a third party. We had received various anonymous calls from suppliers offering us both petrol and diesel at rates that would have guaranteed us a profit and if we had acquiesced, candidly, I doubt Estate Oil would have been any the wiser. I wasn't in the least bit tempted because once you start down that road you never know where it's going to lead. Still, I was extremely frustrated. We were losing money and, almost as irritatingly, trying to find a solution to the problem was taking up a considerable amount of my time. I visited Estate in Dublin and they visited us in Churchtown, but to no avail. I found out that their ten-year contract had subsequently been disallowed under EU legislation, but when I raised this with them they pointed out that this was for new agreements and they had a second charge on the property, and said that if I broke the terms of the agreement they would sue.

Such was the unhappy state of affairs when I ran into Seán Lewis, the Estate Oil area representative, in the Ballyhea petrol station at 5.30 p.m. on Friday 22 April 2005. I imagine it was his last call of the day, for he seemed in a hurry. I was certainly not in the mood to linger because I wanted to get back to Dublin in time for dinner. Nevertheless, I thought it only fair to tell him that we had reached a decision about our future relationship with Estate:

Me: I'm fed up. When our ten-year contract is up in November 2006 you can be certain I won't be renewing it.
Seán: I know you're unhappy, but you won't find any of our competitors offering better terms.
Me: If that turns out to be true then I'm going to become completely independent. I won't have anyone's sign over the forecourt, apart from my own.
Seán: Well, all I'll say is if you do that you'll lose all credibility. You'll have no credibility on the road. You'll have no brand.

The words 'you'll have no brand' had an electrifying effect on me. I had been in marketing for decades. Indeed, such business successes as I had enjoyed had been the result of my ability to create and build brands. In a split second I knew exactly what I was going to do.

Me (to myself): I'm going to create my own brand. In fact, I am going to start my own oil company.
Seán: Have a good weekend.

6

LOVE AT FIRST THOUGHT

In 2005, Irish petrol and diesel sales were worth billions of euros a year and were, thanks to a buoyant economy, growing. The number of petrol stations, however, was falling. In the previous two-year period about one hundred had closed down, bringing the total down to fewer than two thousand, and they were continuing to close. The market was fiercely competitive, not least because the retail giant Tesco had started selling fuel at discounted prices in order to bring more customers into its supermarkets. Indeed, market conditions were such that one of the biggest oil companies in the world, Shell, had decided to pull out of Ireland and was in the process of selling its retail and distribution business to a new operator called Topaz. Statoil, another large player, also ended up selling to Topaz.

I knew none of this at the time. Naturally, I was aware that our own petrol station was struggling to make money, but I attributed our difficulties entirely to the contract that tied us to Estate Oil, which was unfair in that the Estate deal was really the norm rather than the exception. If I had understood the bigger picture, it wouldn't have made any difference to my plans. Come hell or high water I was going to start my own oil company. Seán Lewis had inspired me when he had suggested that without a national brand I would have no credibility. Later, of course, I began to think about the financial advantages of breaking free from Estate and striking out on my own. But it was irritation, not gain, that initially got my creative juices flowing.

For me the creative process is largely about asking 'What if?' questions. What if we reneged on our existing supply contract? What if we talked other tied petrol station owners into joining forces with us? The secret of success when planning any new venture is to not be afraid to explore seemingly ridiculous ideas. It is important – especially in the early stages – to believe that anything is possible. Doubt, reality, logic and practicality destroy innovation. Allowing the chill wind of irrefutable fact to cool my ardour would have been fatal. Leaving aside the state of the market, we were clearly not in a good position to launch an oil company: we had no real experience of the industry and I was fully occupied with my other businesses and not-for-profit work. Furthermore, an oil company demands vast amounts of capital. It needs capital to acquire or build infrastructure; when Shell sold its local distribution depots, oil importation facilities and service stations they were valued at more than €100 million. It also needs capital to purchase the fuel it is going to sell on; my guess is that Shell Ireland, with about 12 per cent of the market, had probably required tens of millions of euros in working capital to fulfil its day-to-day cash demands. Although I was doing well, I was definitely not in that sort of league or anywhere close to it.

Yet, despite all the reasons why thinking about launching an oil company was a waste of time, I thought of little else. I thought of it on the drive home and again the moment I woke up the following day. Indeed, the only thing I wanted to do that Saturday was to put my ideas down on paper and draw up a 'to do' list. I still have a copy of that list:

- Name?
- Register web domain names (.ie, .co.uk, .com)
- Form company (plc?)
- Develop financial projections
- Brief logo and corporate identity
- Legal agreements (keep them simple)
- Brochure/website
- Office back-up (Churchtown)
- Design manual
- Recruit one marketing executive

- Mail shot test
- Decide on business model roll-out

Across the bottom of the page I wrote, 'Remember the new signage will probably have to be retrofitted.' You will notice that I was fixated on the marketing. Looking at the list now I am conscious that a child of ten could have suggested any number of other, more important, issues that I had failed to consider. Happily, I didn't show it to a child of ten, leaving me free to blunder on wholly ignorant of the obvious problems ahead.

The fact is, I was in love, and in the way of lovers everywhere, not only did the object of my affection seem perfect in every conceivable way, I was also confident that I could overcome every obstacle in my path. There may be cold, calculating entrepreneurs out there who don't become emotionally engaged in their businesses. I am certainly not one of them. I don't want to stretch the analogy too far but I must add that in the case of my oil company it was love at first thought. The idea came to me complete and, although I made adjustments here and there along the way, hardly anything changed between when I launched the business and when I sold it three years later. It was based on a simple but powerful concept, which was to contact other petrol station owners in the same precarious and infuriating position as myself – owners who were being forced by one or other of the big oil companies to buy fuel at inflated prices – and to suggest that we join forces. As a single entity we would have the power to obtain fuel at lower, more competitive prices. I intended to provide them with a brand to put on their signs and pumps and to make their forecourts look as good as anything on offer from the big oil companies. Furthermore, instead of tying them to a restrictive contract I planned to give them the strongest of all incentives to remain involved: equity. It had occurred to me that if the other petrol station owners had shares in the new oil company they would have a compelling reason to give it their custom. I had thought of something else, too, that I felt would add to the new venture's credibility. I knew from my studies a few years earlier that if a company had eight shareholders or more and issued a minimum of €40,000 of paid-up share capital it was entitled to call itself a public limited company or 'plc'. Most multinational oil companies had plc status and I decided that our new venture would too.

Once, an old friend came to me with an idea for a business. He wanted me to start it and fund it and simply give him a share for having devised the concept. I liked the idea, so I agreed. It soon transpired, though, that we each had a different perception of what his idea was worth. He believed that it entitled him to a half or, at the bare minimum, a third of the shares. I was unwilling to give him more than 5 per cent. In my experience there is no shortage of good ideas. Only two things count when it comes to launching a new business: execution and capital. It is the people who have the energy and drive to make a business happen, and the people who risk their cash investing in it, who deserve the greatest reward.

I had conceived our oil company as a quasi-confederation or hybrid co-operative. So I set aside 40 per cent of the shares for my fellow petrol station owners. This left 60 per cent for me, any external investors and my team. As the business developed and new people became involved the proportion of shares held by each of the interested parties changed, but I never expected to be rewarded with more than a nominal percentage for my initial brainwave. It was my cash investment and effort that entitled me to shares. The launch team, incidentally, consisted of my fellow directors, Michelle Gleeson and Maurice Gilbert, and myself. Michelle was already looking after all my day-to-day operations and as Maurice had helped me with various Churchtown renewal projects I felt he would have a useful contribution to make. They both also had an equity interest in the Ballyhea petrol station, which was another reason they deserved to be involved. I don't think either of them would be offended if I said that when I was dreaming up the whole scheme they knew as little about the oil sector as I did.

A few days after I had decided to launch my oil company I travelled to New York with friends to participate in the Five Boro Bike Tour. I was there in body but not in spirit. On the flight, during the rain-soaked cycle itself and even while socialising my mind was awhirl with thoughts relating to my new business. I remember trying to interest two of my friends with the name and logo on a cab trip from our hotel to Balthazar restaurant one night, but to no avail. I am sure my friends viewed me with a sort of tolerant pity for thinking about work when we were on holiday. Entrepreneurs are like artists in this respect – always worrying away at their creations. Before I headed off to New York I had chosen a name for the new venture: GreatGas. The name had a double meaning, which I liked. 'Gas' is, of course, the American term for petrol and in Ireland we use it colloquially to mean entertaining or outstanding. Best of all, the Irish often couple it with the word 'great', as in: 'We had a brilliant time. It was great gas altogether.' I felt the name was both Irish and international, had positive connotations and would be easy to remember. Martin Keaney, a graphic designer I had worked with for many years, liked the name too, and immediately started sending me different logo options. Within a fortnight of my meeting with Seán Lewis I had finalised the corporate identity. I had also set up the public company, bought the .com domain name from an American who had previously registered it, and written a short business plan.

Every day I did something else to move the project forward. Early on I started work on the legal agreement between the company and the fuel station owners, whom I decided to call members. I decided not to use a solicitor for this agreement, preferring to write it myself in plain English. I am proud to say that whatever problems we may have encountered at GreatGas the membership agreement was never an issue. It had an interesting section in it, too, that helped me to lock in my members in a way that I knew they wouldn't object to. This was a real issue for me because without a restrictive contract in place there was always a risk that members would buy from me one day and not the next. My solution was to allow them to resign their membership at any time – and buy their fuel wherever they wanted – providing they immediately took down and returned their GreatGas signage, which I was paying for. This signage would be supplied to them free of charge and would, if they wanted, incorporate their own name, as in 'Jack Murphy's GreatGas'. Replacing signage is an expensive business and I felt that this was a wholly reasonable way of ensuring that members didn't take advantage of me.

It is impossible to overstate how ignorant I was about the oil industry. I had ordered a market research document entitled *Irish Service Stations 2004*, which contained no more than some basic statistics.

I had also forwarded my business plan to a Dublin neighbour, Peter O'Donoghue, who had previously worked as a senior executive in Statoil. He was frank. His email response to me opened with the words 'I'll play the part of the wet blanket', after which he set out some powerful reasons why I shouldn't dream of getting into fuel retailing, including:

- *The enormous difficulty of obtaining and providing credit*: It would be nigh on impossible for me to get it and many of the individual operators I hoped to attract as members would be unable to find the money to pay off their existing suppliers before switching to GreatGas.
- *Logistics*: Getting fuel delivered to individual operators all over the country would be expensive and problematic.
- *Establishing standards*: It would require substantial resources to ensure that all the GreatGas operators were observing health and safety regulations, behaving in an environmentally sensitive way and offering high-quality service.
- This was a *highly competitive marketplace* in which it was almost impossible to make money.

Peter's points were invaluable and helped me when it came to planning my business model. He said something else that resonated with me: 'See how many decent-size operators would change over to you.' Of course, my biggest disadvantage when planning how to disrupt a small section of the Irish transport fuel sector – the fact that I knew so little about it – was also my greatest strength. I looked at the industry with completely new eyes. There's a long tradition of entrepreneurs with no experience in a particular market managing to achieve notable success. A good example (and I only wish I was a tiny fraction as innovative) is Richard Branson and the way he shook up the airline industry when he launched Virgin Atlantic. Naturally, I had to learn about the industry I proposed to enter, but I came at it with no preconceived ideas about what would and wouldn't work.

It never ceases to surprise me how skills that are learned in one situation turn out to be useful in another. In the mid-1980s I helped persuade a dubious executive at Bank of Ireland that we should change our advertising strategy. Up until then the bank, in line with all the other financial institutions, had spent its money on generating 'awareness'. Primarily we produced 'feel-good' television commercials, radio commercials and press advertisements designed to make prospects and customers aware of our services. This was fine as far as it went, but it didn't really drive business through our doors. So I suggested that we switch a considerable portion of our annual budget to direct marketing. The main principle of direct marketing is that all your advertising will generate a direct response. For a bank that response might be, for example, a phone call, a completed account opening form or a branch visit. The real point is that the approach produces a measurable result. This in turn allows the advertiser to test different approaches to see what works best. In the 1980s direct marketing experts were terribly excited about something called 'dry testing'. This involves running an advertisement for a product or service you hadn't actually developed to see how the public reacted. If they ordered in droves, you knew you were on to a good thing. On the other hand, if the response was poor you could drop the idea with minimal loss.

I applied the principle of dry testing to my oil company idea. I bought a list of 1,600 petrol stations and on 8 June 2005, just 47 days into my new business, I wrote to their owners and asked them to join me. In this way I hoped to get a feel for whether my idea was feasible. The mailing cost me €3,749 – the price of a decent family holiday for four people. I make that particular comparison because just before the mailing was put into the post I took my family off for a decent family holiday. I hoped that while I was away there would be sufficient response to justify moving forward.

7

WE COULD JUST BE IN BUSINESS

I never imagined that quite so many of the petrol station owners of Ireland would take me at my word when I wrote:

> This communication will be your ONLY chance to find out about GreatGas as there will be no follow up, no hard sell phone calls and no representatives visiting you. We know you are really busy so if you don't respond to this we won't bother you again. You now have the information you need.

My letter summarised the proposition in three paragraphs. First, I explained who we were, and what we planned to do:

> GreatGas has been developed by people like you who own a fore-court. Our business is located on the N20 at Ballyhea, just south of Charleville and not far from the Cork/Limerick county bound-ary. We are shortly coming to the end of a 'tied' relationship and in the future will be operating independently and re-branding as GreatGas.

Next, I explained the concept:

> We know how hard it is to remain motivated selling petrol and diesel at uncompetitive prices dictated by your supplier. That's

why we are convinced that the best possible solution is for a group of independent forecourt owners to establish a professional national brand and then combine our purchasing power. That is what GreatGas is all about. With your support it really will be a case of GreatGas altogether!

Finally, I summarised the benefits:

Are you as concerned as us about the future of petrol and diesel forecourt retailing? Do you want to be independent and yet look really professional? Do you want to sell at competitive prices and still be rewarded with a profit for providing an essential service? If you are like us, then you need to read all about GreatGas and our mission to stop petrol retailers like us making nothing from all our hard work.

The accompanying brochure provided a few extra details, but not that many. I wasn't holding out or keeping anything back; I simply didn't know quite how things would evolve. The mailing was, after all, merely an attempt to gauge interest. Nevertheless, around 80 individuals, a respectable 5 per cent of the petrol station owners I had contacted, replied. This may not sound like an overwhelming response, but given that it was a completely new concept I was more than satisfied. Anyway, there were only so many enquiries that Maurice, Michelle and I could handle.

What this response told me, incidentally, was that we were by no means alone. It was the well-known boiling frog story (put a frog in hot water and it will jump straight out; put it in cold water and heat the water slowly and it will be boiled to death before it realises it is in mortal danger), with the forecourt owners cast as the frog and the wholesale fuel providers as the water heaters.

There was another issue, too, that had to be addressed when I returned from my family holiday. It was Michelle who first voiced it, while she was sending out acknowledgement letters to the people who had been in touch with us.

Michelle (licking the flap of an envelope): Gerry?
Me: Yes?
Michelle (folding a piece of paper): I don't want to sound silly ...
Me: And I'm sure you won't.
Michelle (licking the flap of an envelope): I was just wondering ...
Me: Wondering ...?
Michelle (folding a piece of paper): If you had given any thought at all to where we are going to get our hands on a large quantity of reasonably priced fuel?

As it happened I had been giving it a great deal of thought, but hadn't yet come up with anything vaguely resembling a solution or – to be absolutely accurate – anything vaguely resembling the name of a potential supplier. I had managed, however, to develop what I hoped would prove to be a workable business model.

Leaving aside the question of where to source our fuel, my main problems, as Peter O'Donoghue had wisely predicted, were how to arrive at an easy-to-understand pricing structure that would save my members money and produce a profit for GreatGas, and finding the capital necessary to fund buying and selling what could quickly become millions of euros of fuel a month.

With regard to pricing, as I have explained, all the other Irish oil companies were using complicated formulae generally involving mysterious short-term discounts. One day the discount could be €0.072 per litre, the next €0.10. It was, therefore, close to impossible for tied petrol station owners to accurately calculate their margins. As part of my general industry research I discovered that when fuel was sold in bulk on the international markets the price was usually based on something called 'Platts'. Platts is a specialist information provider that produces market and pricing data for a wide range of commodities. Every day Platts publishes spot prices for petrol and diesel. I decided that GreatGas would supply its members with fuel based on the Platts price plus an agreed margin. This would mean that members would know on any given day exactly what they were paying for fuel. It provided certainty where no certainty had existed before.

It also provided me with an answer to another question that had been troubling me: how was GreatGas going to turn a profit? It came to me in one of those wonderful but only too rare flashes of inspiration that if we worked on the basis of Platts plus margin I could simply add in an agreed per-litre commission to GreatGas. When I started playing with the figures I calculated that GreatGas could probably make a reasonable income by adding just €0.005 per litre. Later I had to increase this, but compared to the other operators we always represented extraordinary value. How did we survive with such a slender margin? Natural modesty prevents me from describing it as a masterstroke, but it occurred to me that I could overcome the need for a distribution network as well as the large sums of capital that would be required to give my members credit by the straightforward expedient of making it our supplier's responsibility. This would lead to an extremely simple business model:

- GreatGas would negotiate with a single supplier, which would have the exclusive right to sell fuel to the members.
- The members could withdraw at any time without notice, provided they immediately took down and returned the GreatGas signage.
- The fuel supplier would sell to members at the Platts price plus an agreed margin and an agreed commission to GreatGas.
- The fuel supplier would provide individual members with credit and would handle all the invoicing.
- The forecourt owner would provide a bank credit guarantee to the supplier.
- The fuel supplier would organise delivery of the fuel.
- GreatGas would invoice the fuel supplier for commission at an agreed rate for every litre sold to its members.

The beauty of this model was that I could set up a virtual oil company with minimal investment. GreatGas wouldn't have to establish distribution centres, buy tankers, pay for massive quantities of fuel or offer credit. As I saw it, the company could be run with a tiny overhead – a small office in Churchtown and a couple of members of staff – and without exposure to substantial risk.

If I had learned one thing from my years in banking, it was that it pays to talk to people face to face. You can send your customers detailed questionnaires, write them long letters and speak to them on the telephone, with good results, but nothing is as productive as a meeting. It takes shared experiences – even if those experiences are no more than sitting either side of a desk – to create a relationship. Such a relationship works to everyone's advantage: more business and valuable information for the seller; greater respect and better deals for the buyer. I mention this because I believe relationship building is no longer considered important by many businesses. They view it as an expensive, unproductive luxury. My own experience is that while it may not yield short-term gains, over time it results in a stronger, healthier, more profitable organisation. I have also noticed that as entrepreneurs and managers become increasingly successful they have less and less time to interact with their customers.

We went out of our way to telephone, visit and, above all else, listen to GreatGas's potential customers, or, as we preferred to think of them, members. It involved a certain amount of counselling. Clearly, my mailing had touched a nerve, but that wasn't enough for me. I was basing the whole business on my experiences with Estate and Ballyhea. Before investing further time and money I wanted to make sure that my suppositions were accurate. As a result of this additional research I not only gained an insight into what other petrol station owners thought but also found the key to the whole enterprise. The breakthrough actually occurred when I visited one of our enquirers – Diarmuid O'Donovan – who, with his mother, ran a petrol station and shop just west of Cork City. The O'Donovans were out of contract and were buying their fuel from a haulier who had effectively set himself up as a wholesale fuel intermediary.

'Where does he get the fuel from, then?' I asked.

'Oh, ConocoPhillips, of course', came the nonchalant reply.

Subsequently, I discovered that ConocoPhillips was one of the world's largest oil and gas exploration and production companies, but at the time I had barely heard of them.

'Remind me where they're based?'

'Whitegate.'

I certainly knew where Whitegate was. The only oil refinery in Ireland, it is located in Cork Harbour opposite Passage West, where the River Lee meets the open sea, less than an hour's drive from Churchtown. It was, literally, the work of ten minutes to look up the name of the company's CEO, Neil O'Carroll, and to write him a short, business-like letter. 'We are interested', I explained, 'in buying €500 million of fuel.' In a way, it is a sort of miracle that he ever read it, let alone answered it. He can't have had any idea who I was and even if he had I don't imagine that he would have been that impressed. True, I had a few other businesses to my name, but as far as the billion-euro Irish fuel market was concerned I was the part-owner of a single, rural petrol station. Afterwards, I never could quite summon up the courage to ask him why he had taken me seriously because I always suspected he was asking himself the same question. Perhaps it was just innate good manners: 'That Murphy chap from Churchtown (wherever that may be) has written to me so, out of politeness, I must write back.' Then again, perhaps Neil O'Carroll recognised a good idea while I was still struggling with the logistics. Whatever the reason, Neil asked Michelle and me in for a meeting and, although nothing was agreed then and there, we came away saying to each other, 'We could just be in business.'

8

IN WHICH EVERYONE IS SURPRISED

'A good plan executed now', according to General George S. Patton, 'is better than a perfect plan executed next week.' I couldn't agree more. As soon as I was certain that I had a workable concept I didn't waste any time trying to finesse it but focused instead on making things happen. I had obtained a quotation for retro-fitting new signage to a typical petrol station and knew that the cost would be anything from €15,000 to €30,000, depending on size and loca-tion. As I had set my heart on a minimum of 100 GreatGas forecourts (in other words up to 5 per cent of the Irish market), I would require between €1.5 million and €3 million to pay for the branding alone. Let me say, quite candidly, that I did not have between €1.5 million and €3 million available. It had also begun to dawn on me after my initial meeting with ConocoPhillips that, refreshing as my lack of experience in the oil sector was, to me anyway, there were some worrying gaps in my knowledge. I decided to seek both additional expertise and capital.

The first step towards this goal was to create a business plan. Everyone has a different idea of what constitutes a business plan. Generally speak-ing, it contains extensive information regarding opportunity, market, competition, strategy, investment, return, cash flow and so forth, not to mention a step-by-step description of how the enterprise will be launched and developed. As anyone involved in writing and carrying out a business plan knows only too well, the scenario it describes in minute detail is the one scenario that will never occur. Why not? In a nutshell – life gets in the way. As Niels Bohr, the Danish physicist, said: 'Prediction is very difficult, especially if it's about the future.' One of the main purposes of a business plan is to persuade people who haven't been directly involved in writing it to devote either time or, more likely, money to the project.

I am not saying that business plans aren't a good idea in and of themselves. The process definitely focuses the minds of everyone involved on the core issues and, if properly prepared, provides a useful action list. Nor must it be forgotten that years later one will derive considerable amusement from rereading the plan and marvelling at one's total naivety and lack of foresight. Some of the most entertaining and amusing things I have ever read have been my old business plans. What I am trying to say is that they are valuable, but it is naive to set too much store by them.

The first proper business plan I prepared for GreatGas had brevity in its favour. It was dated 22 June 2005 and ran to just six pages, including a rather natty cover sheet with an illustration of an imagined GreatGas forecourt and a single page of financial projections. In this document I sketched out the idea, listed off the achievements to date (which were not inconsiderable, given that I had only been working on the business part-time for eight weeks) and suggested that if GreatGas did manage to sign up 100 outlets it would generate an annual operating profit, after overhead costs, of approximately €1.1 million. I sent the plan out to a selection of industry luminaries and organisations that I thought might see cross-over opportunities. For example, I approached Musgrave, the group that controls the Centra and SuperValu chains of supermarkets, with the thought that we might work together. Additionally, I contacted my competitors, commercial property developers, venture capitalists and others. This generated meetings but no concrete results. As the summer progressed, prudence dictated that I reconsider my position.

My family tease me about the way I sometimes change my mind without warning. 'But yesterday you said …' one or another of them will remind me when I unexpectedly alter my stance on a particular subject. 'Ah,' I reply, 'but that was yesterday.' It isn't, as they well know, inconsistency on my part. Occasionally, the only way to test an idea or course of action is to act 'as if' and see how it feels. Also, should some new fact come to light, or if further reflection causes one to see something from a different perspective, one shouldn't be ashamed to make a U-turn. By the end of August 2005 I realised that my business model had some flaws in it, but I didn't think they would prove fatal. True, I had some potential GreatGas members lined up and negotiations with ConocoPhillips were proceeding well. However, no one from within the oil industry had stepped forward to offer his or her services and, of greater concern, there wasn't any serious investor interest, either.

I took to playing with the figures, trying out different scenarios and options. My objective was to find a way of starting the business with a relatively small amount of seed capital and then using the profits to fund further growth. Eventually, I hit on an approach that I felt had a chance of working. It was based on something that had been patently obvious from day one: GreatGas would take time to build. Most of our members would first have to disengage themselves from their existing tied arrangements or wait until their contract had expired before they could sign up with us. I wasn't going to enrol my 100 petrol stations overnight, which meant I wasn't going to need anywhere near the capital I had first anticipated. Moreover, once we were established I felt that members would accept that they had to pay for some or even all of the rebranding themselves. Indeed, I decided that to begin with we would only grant aid the first twenty stations, limiting our investment to €10,000 per new member. On this basis it seemed to me that €200,000 would see us through the initial launch period. Using my personal savings and with the help of a bank loan, €200,000 was within my means.

I have mentioned that negotiations with ConocoPhillips were proceeding well. Despite their extraordinary size, more than 15,000 employees and tens of billions of dollars of revenue a year, they negotiated with us as if we were equals. I have to admit that as the part-owner of a single, unprofitable petrol station I found the whole experience slightly surreal. The senior executive handling matters for ConocoPhillips was Paul Barrington. During meetings, I frequently saw a deeply puzzled expression cross his face, as if he couldn't quite believe he was bothering with anything so small and insignificant. Still, with no more than the to-be-expected amount of haggling, we agreed prices, commission, delivery and – crucially – credit terms for the members. With regard to the last of these, ConocoPhillips granted credit to any of our members willing (and able) to put a bank guarantee in place. This was a major concession; not all suppliers would have been as generous and it made it possible to start rolling out the business.

The one sticking point was my desire for a joint press release. This was clearly to GreatGas's advantage and the moment the draft contract had been signed off in late September 2005 I proposed a joint press release with the dramatic headline 'GreatGas enters long-term supply agreement with ConocoPhillips'.

Using an approach one associates more with the Japanese than the Americans, ConocoPhillips managed to avoid saying 'yes' to a press release without actually saying 'no'. For months I submitted different versions to them in the hope that eventually their PR department, which was based in Houston, Texas, would agree to some sort of public statement. It would have tickled me to see the name of my minnow of an oil company connected, in print, with such a colossus, and I am sure it would have helped bring in new members. However, it was not to be. The Irish office used to send each draft to the Houston office, who would sit on it for weeks before replying. I imagine that the conversation at ConocoPhillips HQ must have gone something like this:

> *Press Officer One*: That guy Murphy in Ireland has been on again about a joint press release.
> *Press Officer Two*: He's determined; I'll say that for him.
> *Press Officer One*: Usual response?
> *Press Officer Two*: Yep. Wait a fortnight and then tell him we can't approve it in its current form and that before he sends anything to the media we have to agree it.

It had never been my intention to renege on the contractual arrangement between my own petrol station at Ballyhea and Estate. I had known about the contract when I bought Ballyhea and, although I am aware that it will sound a bit sanctimonious – probably because it *is* a bit sanctimonious – I considered that it would be unethical to breach its terms. Having said this, it did seem to me that it would be reasonable to request that Estate Oil sold us fuel at the same price we were being offered by ConocoPhillips. When I contacted Estate to ask for better prices I suppose in my heart of hearts I hoped that they would be difficult, and they were. Not only did they refuse to match the ConocoPhillips prices but for two weeks they failed to take any calls or reply to any emails. Then, out of the blue, they rang with a price increase for diesel and a negligible reduction for petrol. I had had enough. On 6 October I bought €37,837.18 worth of fuel from ConocoPhillips for Ballyhea. On 10 October Michelle wrote to Estate ending the relationship, closing her letter with a paragraph that delighted me, even if it didn't delight them: 'We are de-branding our station from 17th to 28th October. Please advise where you wish us to return the totem pole, fascia and all the other Estate signage.' Estate Oil rather bows out of the story at this juncture except for the fact that, in the end, we – rightly so – compensated them in full for the loss they suffered as a result of Ballyhea walking away from the contract one year early. There were no hard feelings and we wished Estate well going forward.

The official launch date for GreatGas was Sunday 13 November 2005. Maurice, Michelle and I had our photographs taken in front of the pumps at Ballyhea a few days beforehand and a press release (in which no reference was made to our main fuel supplier) was distributed to the media. The opening actually received a surprising amount of newspaper, radio and television coverage. This was not because editors were excited to discover that a new player had entered the retail petrol market, but because we used the occasion to make a very different sort of announcement: 'First forecourt in Ireland to retail PPO biofuel to general public'.

The first person to think of using vegetable oil as a form of fuel was, strangely enough, Rudolf Diesel, the inventor of the engine that bears his name. He began experimenting with it in the early 1900s and during a speech in 1912 he said, 'The fact that fat oils from vegetable sources can be used may seem insignificant today, but such oils may perhaps become in course of time of the same importance as some natural mineral oils and the tar products are now.' Diesel was, of course, ahead of his time. Thanks to the availability of relatively inexpensive mineral oil, there was little interest in a natural alternative. However, after the millennium, as people began to become concerned about global warming and oil prices started to rise, vegetable oil moved back onto the agenda. In Ireland there was the added incentive of not wanting to be wholly dependent on imported fuel. It was widely accepted that in the event of a world energy crisis Ireland would be in an extremely vulnerable position.

True, only a handful of Irish drivers had actually adapted their vehicles to run on the fuel, which they often processed themselves from used cooking oil. On the other hand, a group of farmers in Wexford had started a rapeseed oil refinery and a growing number of engineers offered to convert existing diesel vehicles so that they could run on either type of fuel for as little as €1,600. I think it's fair to say that by 2005 the concept had entered the Irish subconscious, promoted by frontier people like Allen Holman. In light of these factors, Irish-produced pure plant oil (PPO) biofuel made perfect sense. It was cheaper than diesel, there being no duty to pay on it; it took just 30,000 miles (48,000 kilometres) of driving to fully pay back the capital costs involved in adapting a diesel engine; and being a natural lubricant it prolonged the life of the engine. It made environmental sense, too. PPO biofuel delivers the same power and economy as diesel with the benefit of zero carbon emissions. Moreover, it is biodegradable and doesn't cause water or air pollution. As the first petrol station to distribute PPO biofuel we became media darlings. Indeed, I was so convinced that we were selling the fuel of the future that we invested €20,000 in an extra overground PPO tank and pump at Ballyhea. We also had our shop van upgraded so that it could use the fuel. I built PPO biofuel into our business plan and envisioned that all the GreatGas members would sell it alongside petrol and diesel.

As an aside, apart from GreatGas, surprisingly Ballyhea is also where another national franchise was created. The Wine Buff was created by Ballyhea man Paddy O'Flynn in 2000. Paddy, who is based in Saint-Émilion in Bordeaux, was a former manager of La Tour des Vins, one of the premier wine shops in Saint-Émilion, and he has leveraged his expertise to create a franchise from scratch with over a dozen outlets in Ireland. The Wine Buff and GreatGas are, as Mel Brooks might say, 'world famous in Ballyhea'.

9

BETWEEN THE CRISPY DUCK AND THE KUNG PAO CHICKEN

Trying to persuade consumers and GreatGas members to support PPO biofuel turned out to be something of, if not a red herring, certainly a green one. At the time I believed it had a major role to play in Irish transport, but I was concerned about the lack of suppliers. Essentially, there was only one PPO refinery in the country and if the farmers running it ever decided to close down the operation (which could easily happen if they found that they could make more money growing a different crop) there would be no alternative source. Accordingly, I began to research the idea of a Churchtown-based, GreatGas-sponsored PPO refinery. I envisioned a state-of-the-art facility that would produce fuel and, using the waste matter, a natural animal feed too.

I was keen on PPO, Maurice and Michelle were keen, the media were keen; but our customers were not. Although drivers liked the idea when polled, few were actually willing to spend the money required to adapt their vehicles for its use. Many were also put off by the fact that there was only one forecourt in the entire country where the fuel could be purchased: Ballyhea. We fared no better with other petrol station owners. GreatGas members were not unenthusiastic to begin with. However, when they realised that it was going to cost up to €20,000 to put in the necessary tank and pump, with little or no chance of a return on their investment for many years to come, not one stepped forward to become the second forecourt in Ireland to retail PPO biofuel to the public. Eventually, however, with the help of an EU grant, in time we did persuade three other forecourt owners to install overground tanks in order that they, too, could sell PPO.

It was a classic chicken and egg situation. My colleagues and I promoted it as best we could for a year or so and then, reluctantly, let it drop. This failure was, incidentally, the only real disappointment I experienced with regard to any aspect of GreatGas. I won't pretend that I didn't take it hard. It was satisfying to feel that I was shaking up the retail fuel market and helping small businesses to prosper. It would have been much more satisfying to have been doing something that would have really helped Ireland and, in a modest way, the planet. That 'better to have tried and failed than never to have tried at all' stuff is all very well, but there have been a few occasions in my life where I desperately wanted to win, and making a success of PPO biofuel was one of them.

I must just make one other comment about my foray into PPO biofuel. We received, as I have intimated, a good deal of media attention. You may think that this was a good thing, and by and large it was, but it had a quite unexpected consequence. Potential customers were bypassing the Ballyhea service station under the entirely erroneous impression that we didn't sell any other type of fuel. Heaven knows how much business we lost because of this, but it was a good lesson to learn. In principle, all publicity is good publicity. In practice, it can sometimes backfire.

Anyway, the GreatGas PPO biofuel fiasco was still in the future in the run-up to Christmas 2005, when I was focusing entirely on how best to capitalise on the enquiries we kept receiving from potential GreatGas members. I felt somewhat stretched. On top of all my usual work, I was preparing for the launch of *The Annals of Churchtown*. I am under no illusions about the wider appeal of this extremely detailed slice of local history, but it was important to me and, because it had absorbed so much of my time, it spurred me to look for someone to take over GreatGas. In November I ran an advertisement in the national media for a business development executive. The successful candidate's first task would be to 'develop a branded member network of 100 forecourts by 2010'.

Although it was a decent-sized advertisement and appeared in several publications (I know this because looking at the accounts I see that I spent over €3,000 placing it), the idea of working for a start-up in an out-of-the way village in north Cork did not, it transpired, have universal appeal and just seven people responded. I drew up an initial short list of … one. Ray O'Sullivan had obtained an MBA while in full-time employment (as I had done) and seemed to be a good candidate, but he didn't have any relevant industry experience, having worked in agrichemicals for most of his career. Yet, as our conversation unfolded, I found more and more to like about him.

I had decided before I met Ray that I was going to offer him the job and, to sweeten the deal, I suggested that he be paid a combination of salary and shares so that if we hit our business goal of 100 forecourts he would own a significant stake in the business. Interestingly, he was less concerned with his share options than with his title: 'If I am to be really effective I must be the managing director. Otherwise, the forecourt owners I am speaking to won't respect me. I'll just be another rep.' It was a compelling argument, and I agreed.

The board meeting to appoint Ray was held on the evening of 11 January 2006 in the Golden Mill Chinese Restaurant in Kilmallock. At some point between the crispy duck and the Kung Pao chicken we passed a resolution that Ray would become managing director as of 6 February.

According to my copy of the agenda, which is slightly splattered with what looks like sweet and sour sauce, we discussed rather a lot at that dinner. Another oil wholesaler was offering to supply us, and we were tempted, but in the end we decided that we would rather have an exclusive arrangement with ConocoPhillips. We also discussed signage grants for the members we didn't yet have, our marketing material and our legal paperwork. It was at this meeting we first began to talk about the language we would use to describe what we were doing. I liked the words 'member', 'shareholder' and 'co-operative' because they all suggested inclusivity. We wanted our GreatGas members to feel that we were all in this together and we decided on:

GreatGas is a branded franchise co-operative buying group, founded in Ireland and operated by a team of fuel forecourt owners.

Another idea that came up at that meeting (it is amazing how conducive Chinese food is to creativity) was to ask the Ballyhea petrol station auditors to produce figures demonstrating how much more profitable our own forecourt trade had become after we had rebranded ourselves as GreatGas. The firm analysed our turnover in the same four weeks of January 2005 and January 2006 and discovered that grocery sales had risen 30 per cent and fuel sales were up a staggering 542 per cent! They worked out that whereas the fuel business had operated at a loss in 2004 and 2005, in 2006 it was expected to achieve a gross margin of 5 per cent. I don't think it is an exaggeration to say that these audited figures were a great deal of help to Ray when he started approaching possible GreatGas members.

I have already said, more than once I am afraid, but I do feel quite strongly about it, that the success of any new venture depends much more on its execution than on the originality of its core concept. I will go further. As an entrepreneur you may as well pack up your tent and steal away into the night if you don't have an effective sales strategy. For me, selling isn't about persuading prospects to buy whatever it is you have on offer – it's about meeting needs. By this I mean listening, responding, building relationships, solving problems, providing information and generally communicating well. Ray turned out to be a past master at all these things, reflected in the speed with which he began to sign up new GreatGas members.

Ray's technique was simple. He got into his car and drove all over the country dropping in on the independent forecourt owners who had contacted us and, if they seemed at all responsive, taking the time to visit them a second or third time. He never pushed himself on anyone. He was quick to address any questions or doubts. And if someone expressed firm interest, he made it as easy as possible for them to switch from whichever supplier they were using to GreatGas. Michelle had already started negotiations with several forecourts, so within a few weeks Ray was able to capitalise on these contacts and he signed up four forecourts, in Skibbereen, Mallow, Youghal and Ballylickey. It was clear that Ray was a star appointment.

It is a testimony to Ray's ability that these new members became the most vociferous advocates for GreatGas. They told other forecourt owners how happy they were with our service and our prices. More than this, they spoke about it to the media. We were regularly being covered in the national, trade and local press and, happily, no one seemed to have anything unkind to say about us. In May 2006, for example, Paul Connolly (GreatGas, Skibbereen) was quoted in a feature as saying, 'I was fed up with never knowing what my fuel was actually costing me. Now, thanks to GreatGas, I know what it costs the day it is delivered and can price accordingly.' In the same article Pat Buckley (GreatGas, Mallow) said, 'We haven't looked back since we switched to GreatGas.'

There are some businesses where you want to appear smaller than you really are or where smallness is considered a positive advantage. Ballyhoura Apple Farm (which I co-own with Maurice Gilbert) is a good example of this. An artisan apple juice producer is generally rated somewhat higher – in terms of product and service quality – than some faceless food corporation. The oil sector, however, is not like this. Size counts. We didn't want to mislead anyone but, on the other hand, we knew that our credibility would be vastly improved if we were seen to be larger than we actually were. When we started with ConocoPhillips, they were delivering fuel in unbranded trucks. About halfway through 2006 it occurred to us that we should ask Michael Hartnett from our delivery company to agree to brand a tanker in the GreatGas colours. The first GreatGas tanker cost us €5,000 to brand and, as no one knew we didn't own it (or the others we subsequently paid to brand), apart from Mick, it definitely gave the impression that we were growing at a rapid pace. I must add, on a purely personal basis, that the first time I saw a GreatGas coming towards me in the road I became so excited I nearly crashed! Another rather cheeky thing we did to create the impression that we were altogether bigger than might otherwise be supposed was to make a television commercial. We ran it on RTE 1 in December 2006 and in it we wished our customers and members the usual season's greetings. If memory serves, our television budget was under €4,000. A tiny price to pay for a great deal of impact.

10

2006: Things Become a Little More Complicated

I suspect it is human nature, or perhaps entrepreneurial nature, to look at other people's businesses and assume that they are simple and straightforward. Even though I have now been starting and managing businesses full time since 1997, I still frequently make the error of underestimating how complex all 'adventures in the nature of trade' actually are. The innumerable difficulties that entrepreneurs face on a daily basis are generally not apparent to the outside world. There are many reasons for this. Most ventures can be described in a few words, thus creating the wholly erroneous impression that they are not terribly complex. Nor is it in a business's interests for the customers and staff to hear about its problems since, should they do so, they may lose confidence in its stability. Moreover, if you aren't closely involved with a particular business on a day-to-day basis, it is impossible to know the thousands of (often minute) decisions required to keep it operating. I think Samuel Butler summarised the reality of business life when he remarked, 'The course of true anything never does run smooth.'

At the end of 2006, if I hadn't been privy to the inner workings of GreatGas, I might have made the mistake of believing that it was enjoying unprecedented success and that its future was assured. In the space of under a year it had attracted a dozen members and was clearly on course for bigger and better things. It had obtained a level of media attention unheard of for such a modest company, especially one operating in a decidedly unglamorous sector, and it was led by a young and

52

efficient managing director who seemed to have a clear sense of direction. A visit to the GreatGas offices in Churchtown would have revealed a lean, professional, hard-working team of just Ray and two part-time employees. As an independent observer I would have admired the company's strategy of outsourcing everything it could, from signage to answering the telephone. Nor, had I looked at the accounts, would I have been surprised to discover that it wasn't making money. After all, it was a start-up and few start-ups move into profit for at least three years.

I was, of course, privy to the inner workings of GreatGas and I have to say that by the end of 2006 the real situation was both favourable and unfavourable. On the plus side it was highly satisfying to know that the business model worked. Without having to expend money on storage capacity, fuel stock, transport, forecourts or any of the other requirements deemed necessary to establish a chain of service stations – in fact, with minimal investment – we had managed to make a significant impact on the market. Moreover, our brand was already recognised countrywide.

On the minus side we were struggling with all sorts of challenges, and failure to deal with any one of them would have spelled instant disaster. There was no certainty during the three years we were building GreatGas that it would survive. At any moment calamity might have struck and all our work would have been in vain. It is always tempting to make light of the effort necessary to create a profitable business. The truth is that we were perpetually snatching victory from the jaws of defeat. Building GreatGas into a €100 million company in three years was not easy.

Ironically, the reason we struggled and the reason we thrived were one and the same: lack of capital. After the initial launch, GreatGas's core problem was that it didn't have sufficient capital to fund its expansion. I knew about the concept of 'over trading' from my branch banking days. Now I was beginning to understand first-hand what experts meant when they talked about how difficult it can be to manage growth. I had previously thought that all growth was, automatically, good news. It transpires that this is only true if you have access to sufficient quantities of cash. Otherwise, there is rarely a moment when one isn't juggling one's resources in order to keep the whole operation from falling apart. Valuable time that would otherwise be devoted to expanding the business is spent chasing debtors, liquidating assets one would rather hold, searching for lenders, being forced to borrow at above-average interest rates, postponing payment to creditors and delaying investments. It means, by turn, begging, apologising and bluffing. It means constant, nagging worry, for no sooner has one dealt with one crisis than one is faced with another.

But if a shortage of capital caused a few cold moments and the odd sleepless night for my colleagues and me, it also spurred us on. We had no spare money so we were careful with what we had. Not a penny was wasted and we thought carefully before we invested in anything. Businesses built in this way tend to be lean and hardy. When money is, to quote the Valentine Brothers' song, 'too tight to mention', it tends to stimulate creativity. We had our backs to the wall and it forced us to come up with ingenious and cost-effective solutions to all our problems. At the time I believed that the business would have expanded much faster had we had funds available, but in hindsight I am not so sure it would have been entirely beneficial. Would we have been so careful about the members we signed up, for example? As the cost of fitting signage to each new GreatGas petrol station was so great, we first made sure that their owners were really committed to us and that they were sound credit risks. Indeed, it wasn't until we had access to capital – that is to say in our fourth year – that we suffered a single bad debt. Maybe there is a lesson in this. I doubt, too, that we would have kept such a tight lid on our cost base if we had had more money at our disposal. The temptation to spend money on higher salaries, extra staff and additional marketing would have been almost irresistible.

Against this, there is no doubt that we missed opportunities to enrol new members because we didn't have the money available to close the deals. We needed the cash not only to fund the signage but also to cover the cost of our fuel deliveries. ConocoPhillips had originally agreed to invoice each of our members separately, and these members had to provide a bank guarantee to ConocoPhillips. Well, in 2006 ConocoPhillips changed its mind. Understandably, the company's credit department wasn't geared up to deal with small, individual accounts and it decided that GreatGas must shoulder the administration and the risk.

This was a dreadful blow. We were able to get the bank guarantees switched across to us relatively easily, but having to carry the risk tied up our capital. As we expanded, the amount we needed got larger and larger. I worried about it constantly.

I don't want to harp on about the stresses and strains that arise from a growing business being insufficiently capitalised, but the subject is one close to my heart. As is so often the case, it never rains but it pours. GreatGas's need for cash occurred at a time when several other businesses and not-for-profit activities I was involved in were also looking for additional funds. After 2007 the situation became really serious, but in 2006 the solution was still relatively easy. We switched banks to one that was willing to lend GreatGas slightly more money. True, it meant signing a large personal seven-figure guarantee, but I was prepared to take the risk.

I should also add that there was a silver lining to the revised ConocoPhillips terms of trade: it forced us to widen our margins. When we originally set the amount of commission we would take on each litre sold to our members, we had had no real idea what our cost base would be. Once we were up and running it was clear that our business model was not sustainable. We simply had to increase our margin on sales. It is an obvious but much forgotten truth that if you have a good relationship with your customers they are likely to be understanding if you need to raise your prices. Our members knew they were receiving a better financial deal with us, our pricing was transparent and our service was second to none.

We enrolled members, of course, as quickly as we dared. That is to say, as quickly as our cash reserves allowed. Although it wasn't a complicated process per se, it did take a good deal of time, which was an issue for a company with only one full-time member of staff: Ray. It fell to him not only to make the sale but also to handle most of the follow-up. His starting point was the paperwork. True, our contract was short and written in plain English but, naturally enough, many prospective members still wanted it checked by their lawyers. By the same token, although they are commonplace, bank guarantees still have to be negotiated. Once the documentation was in place, which could take a couple of months, the forecourt had to be surveyed and design proposals made. Once approved, the work itself had to be arranged and overseen. Companies such as Topaz or Esso have whole departments to deal with these functions; not so for GreatGas. Even after we took on our second full-time employee in 2007, we were perpetually stretched.

We encountered another problem during the early stages of our expansion. Several of the other oil companies decided that we were a threat. Initially, I was rather flattered by the attention. After all, when a multinational deigns to notice your existence and then considers it worth their while to attack you, it is a sign that you are on to something. Our competitors adopted a two-pronged strategy. The first involved undermining us with our potential members. This was very difficult to prove because, of course, no one wanted to come forward and testify, but representatives from a number of oil companies were spreading what can only be described as lies about GreatGas. Ray would call on a prospect only to be told, 'You aren't reliable. I've heard your deliveries fail to turn up', 'Your prices are all very well now, but everyone says that once you've locked in a forecourt you push your prices up' or 'Given your shaky financial position, I'm just not interested.'

The second line of attack was more direct. One multinational, for instance, accused us of enticing their dealers to break their contracts. I denied this, which was easy because it wasn't true, and wrote back, 'We are merely providing all filling stations with the information they require to make an informed decision on where to source product after their contracts have expired.'

I repeatedly wrote letters of complaint to the Competition Authority. Indeed, for much of 2006 letters were flying between the major oil companies, their lawyers, the various regulatory bodies and GreatGas. I remember a particularly vitriolic exchange with a well-known oil distributor, one of the few companies that we could actually prove had defamed us. Its managing director called me on my mobile phone while I was in a supermarket and started verbally abusing me. I laughed it off to begin with, but he kept on shouting and in the end I began to bellow back at him. It is, to the best of my recollection, one of only a few times in my whole career I have lost my temper to such an extent. Heaven knows what the other shoppers must have thought. Afterwards I wrote to threaten legal proceedings, but when I had calmed down I decided I would rather put the money into my business than spend it on lawyers.

Being targeted like this was mildly irritating but it didn't really affect our growth. Anyway, I don't mind being shot at, providing, of course, that the bullets miss – which they did.

11

Decisions, Decisions (Some Good, Some Bad)

I should make it clear that there was nothing hands-on about my involvement with GreatGas. I didn't have time to be anything other than a non-executive chairman, as my diary for 2007, the second year of trading, clearly demonstrates. To begin with, I appear to have taken even more holidays (and I do like my breaks) than usual that year. I was at home with my family for the first week of January, went to India for a two-week tour in March, cycled in Sicily for a week in May and visited Mexico and the USA for three weeks in July.

Not that I was idle between my holidays. GreatGas was just one of around a dozen major projects I was involved with in 2007. These other projects don't form part of this narrative and I only mention them because they explain why I was particularly distracted that year. I had my hands full (although not as full as they were to become in 2008) with, among other things, increasing my stake in Marble & Granite (a company that supplies natural stone and fireplaces) and investing in two start-ups (My Tradesman, a web directory service, and Kendlebell, a franchised virtual office provider). My commitment to Churchtown continued; as I have explained, I had had the idea of raffling a house in order to raise money for a GAA sports hall and as we held the draw in May I was busy with that. I was also in the process of developing the village supermarket and some residential letting properties.

New businesses quickly develop a life of their own. The employees, customers, opening hours, nature of the work and location of the operation are just some of the factors that give any organisation its character. In explaining how GreatGas turned from a €3,749 investment into a €100 million business I am conscious that I have stripped the story down to its bare essentials and, in doing so, haven't really painted a picture of what it was all actually like.

The company was run on a skeleton staff consisting of Ray, two part-time employees and, from around the end of 2007 if memory serves, another full-time salesperson. They all operated out of two large, sunny rooms in the Market House, Churchtown. I had originally converted the building into a hostel and when it was turned into offices I kept a bedroom and bathroom suite for myself to use. I didn't live so much over the business as immediately adjacent to it. Of course, I was only in residence two or three days a week and had little involvement with the day-to-day management of GreatGas, but my presence definitely gave the company's headquarters a slightly domestic feel. At any rate, the atmosphere in the office was informal to the point of homeliness. This was enforced by the business's bucolic location. In every direction it was surrounded by verdant, unspoilt countryside. Rural Ireland does not stand on ceremony and even something as quintessentially conservative as an oil company couldn't fail to be strongly influenced by such pastoral surroundings.

No business exists in a vacuum, and I remember all sorts of events from 2007, none of which had a direct bearing on GreatGas, and yet all of which I associate with the company because they occurred while it was growing in such a dramatic way. In Northern Ireland, for instance, power sharing began again and later the British army ended its longest ever military operation. In the Republic we had a general election and Dan Keating, the oldest man in the country, and a veteran of the Irish War of Independence, died aged 105. I can also recall what the weather was like at different points of the year: January was windy, April dry and warm, June wettish and October cloudy. What I am trying to say is that GreatGas did not exist for me in splendid isolation; rather, it was part of a bigger tableau.

One of the interesting aspects of running any venture, and this includes a company that is growing at breakneck speed, is that the management spends a surprising amount of time making relatively small decisions. When I did talk to Ray or a member of the GreatGas team, it was often about matters of little or no apparent consequence. Which new business leads should be followed up first? Do we need a new office computer? How will operations be affected when one of the three employees goes on annual leave? I found these conversations a useful way of keeping track of what was happening in the business day to day. Furthermore, they often led on to wider discussions: prioritising leads becomes a conversation about growth; the computer becomes a conversation about the role of IT in our business; and so forth. Of course, we frequently wasted time debating irrelevant decisions. In early 2007, to give just one example, ConocoPhillips put the Whitegate Refinery up for sale and Ray and I became quite concerned that if the disposal went through the buyer would either refuse to supply us or substantially change the terms of trade. We were also worried that our members would hear of the proposed sale and, as a result, lose confidence in GreatGas's ability to supply them. After some debate Ray sent a long letter to all our members reassuring them that a change in ownership would not affect us. It was unnecessary. No member ever raised the subject; had we thought it all through we would have realised any future owner would want to retain our business; and, had we waited, it would have become clear that there wasn't going to be a sale. If I had to offer entrepreneurs just one piece of advice, it would be to focus on what is really important.

More by accident than by design, we made a couple of really good (and important) decisions during 2007. Perhaps the wisest of these was not to be overly obsessed with our branding. In the previous year we had been approached by one or two independent forecourt owners keen to buy fuel from us without necessarily becoming GreatGas members. We had obliged them and in 2007 we realised that such independents would allow us to grow faster with minimal capital outlay. This required a readjustment of our own perceptions regarding the business. In my heart of hearts I wanted GreatGas to be a strict, member-only partnership. Such a model would allow us to build closer, stronger relationships with our customers and would simultaneously strengthen our brand. To simply sell fuel to anyone who wanted it seemed to defeat our original purpose. But I overcame my prejudice and the non-member independent forecourts became a valuable source of revenue; they were actually what allowed us to hit the magic €100 million annual turnover figure as we entered our fourth year.

Another good decision we made in 2007 was to sign a deal with LCC Oil, a family-run, Derry-based coal merchant – its full name was Lissan Coal Company Limited – that had branched into motor fuel. I have spoken about how lack of capital was holding back our growth, but there was another problem we hadn't been able to solve. The margins on transport fuel are minuscule. During that period, it cost three cents a litre to haul petrol from Cork to, say, Dublin and this additional expense made supplying anywhere more than about 170 kilometres from the Whitegate Refinery uneconomic for GreatGas. In other words, the location of our sole supplier meant we couldn't take on any members north of Portlaoise. The contract we signed with LCC Oil changed all that. Suddenly, we were able to offer a national service and to expand northwards. We didn't move into Northern Ireland itself because we didn't have the resources to handle the regulatory and currency issues, but we were no longer confined to the southernmost third of the country.

A side benefit to the LCC Oil arrangement was that it meant we were no longer 100 per cent dependent on ConocoPhillips. In 2007 ConocoPhillips sought to put a revised agreement in place and as part of the new arrangement they wanted to cap the number of members we could sign to 35. I could not understand their thinking. I suspect the problem stemmed from the fact that whereas the local management could see the benefit of supporting us, it made less sense to their superiors. The international finance department, in particular, seemed to view GreatGas as high risk and they invested hours and hours every month in chasing us. Indeed, I am certain that the cost of executive time spent by ConocoPhillips worrying about potential (but non-existent) GreatGas losses far outweighed any actual loss they might conceivably have experienced. At any rate, I was glad we had a second supplier in place.

In one respect the ConocoPhillips finance department was not entirely wrong: the GreatGas cash shortage, which had begun in

2006, continued. It distressed me, but not for the reasons you might expect. I knew our overheads were low and under control. We were suffering because we were growing, not because the underlying business was in trouble. At any juncture we could have stopped expanding and moved into profit, but I simply didn't want to stop expanding. My original vision had been to give our members around 40 per cent of the company, but within a few months of our launch I realised that this was impracticable. Members were happy to receive free – or virtually free – shares, but they weren't willing to fund our growth. Under the circumstances 40 per cent was more than they deserved and ultimately they accounted for a more modest (but still generous) share of the equity. I felt, therefore, free to sell shares to an external investor and this was what I had been trying to do, intermittently, since 2006. I can't pretend I approached this in a systematic way. When I thought of an individual or a firm I believed might be interested I would contact them. Most were kind enough to see me, and during 2007 I made several formal presentations.

Nothing came of any of this activity. It wasn't that prospective partners didn't see the potential, but my timing was bad. When I began the search for a partner I wasn't looking for enough money. In Ireland, during the boom years, if you were managing a large investment portfolio, perhaps worth millions of euros, a €250,000 stake in a start-up oil business was too small to be attractive. By the end of 2007 I wondered if I was looking for too little. The economy had slowed dramatically, and although it would be another year before the country officially went into recession, capital was in short supply. I never stopped searching for a partner – indeed, as the company moved towards its third year of trading I redoubled my efforts – but to no avail.

I would like to say that the bank we were with stepped into the breach and helped out. They didn't. We finished 2006 with a turnover of €20 million – not bad for ten months of trading – and it was rising quickly. We were a low-risk account because all our debtors supplied bank guarantees, as had I in my capacity as the founding director. Moreover, we were, if you stripped out capital expenditure, cash positive. It wasn't even as if we were looking for vast sums of money. Nevertheless, our existing bank refused to increase our borrowings over €250,000. By moving our account elsewhere, I was able to obtain a €450,000 facility, but given the company's progress even this was pathetically low.

I can't say we ever solved the cash issue, but we did find ways to alleviate it. With considerable regret we sold the Ballyhea service station and I made my share of the proceeds available to GreatGas. I also made short-term loans to the company of up to €100,000, sometimes putting the money in one day to cover our fuel purchases from ConocoPhillips and taking it out again a few days later. Ray became an investor in the company, too, and thus obtained a 25 per cent stake well before he had reached his 100-member target. Thus by one means or another we managed to sustain our growth as we entered 2008.

12

UNDER ATTACK

By the end of 2007 we were delivering fuel to over thirty service stations a week. Ray was on the verge of closing deals with another dozen or so stations and he was pursuing perhaps a further twenty hot leads. As you can imagine, he was perpetually in transit, driving all over the country to meet with members, customers and prospects. If we had had a complicated business model, trying to look after the needs of so many people would have been impossible. But we didn't have a complicated business model. Essentially, we sold one product: motor fuel. Once a new account was set up there was very little to do except take the orders and pass them on to our own suppliers, ConocoPhillips or LCC. Moreover, we had a compelling story to tell: switch your service station to GreatGas and look forward to lower fuel prices on a long-term, consistent basis. True, we only had a relatively small market share, but after two years of successful trading we had established a relatively high level of credibility. When we had originally launched, some forecourt owners had been sceptical about whether we would be able to survive in such a competitive environment, while others doubted we would be reliable when it came to deliveries. We had proved the pessimists wrong. As we geared up for a major push in early 2008, we had every reason to feel confident that the pace of growth would be increasing and that our target of 100 stations by the end of 2010 was achievable.

Self-belief is such an important attribute in any entrepreneur. From 1998 to 2000 I was a non-executive director at Sherry FitzGerald, now one of Ireland's largest property advisory firms. I saw at first hand the entrepreneurial hand of Mark FitzGerald as he moved Sherry FitzGerald from a Dublin-based business to a property advisory company with branches and agents throughout Ireland. In 1998, Mark and I went to Parsippany in New Jersey to meet the world leader in franchised property brands, Cendant Corporation (since renamed Realogy). Cendant told us they had 'the system' and we could have it if Sherry FitzGerald took on their franchise. It was tempting to buy into their success story because at that time Cendant controlled the ERA, Coldwell Banker and Century 21 real estate franchise brands worldwide and there was no franchised estate agency in the Republic of Ireland. However, Mark was brave and had the entrepreneurial confidence and self-belief to forego the Cendant system and create his own franchise from scratch, Sherry FitzGerald Countrywide.

Our confidence was founded on various factors: growing sales, of course, and the palpable enthusiasm we encountered from forecourt owners, but most of all the deluge of letters of complaint we received from our competitors and their lawyers. We reasoned that multinational oil companies like Esso and Topaz would not threaten legal action if they weren't seriously concerned about the effect we might have on their business. I have an entire filing cabinet drawer full of their missives and our responses, but I will satisfy myself with a few select quotes to give you a flavour of how rattled the big players had become.

To begin with, when a petrol station came out of contract and switched to GreatGas their former suppliers would try all sorts of ruses to stop us delivering to them. Here's a typical attempt:

Take note that if you deliver product to the site in question during the next 60 days our client will take legal action against your company and will look to you for damages and costs.

Interestingly, not a single legal action was taken against us.

Even after a multinational had lost a customer to GreatGas, it would still do its best to hamper us. Here's a paragraph from a letter sent to us by another company:

> It has come to our attention that the above service station is in the process of removing the brand signage provided by us ... and replacing the same with GreatGas signage. We require an undertaking from you by return that your company will not supply the site ... if your company has removed our signage same must be returned without delay.

One company took a more aggressive line. They decided to attack us on the grounds that we were trying to lure their customers away by informing them of our lower prices and better terms. Their lawyers kicked off a bizarre legal threat with the following attempt to frighten us:

> Our client ... has informed us that you are contacting dealers who have exclusive motor fuel supply agreements with our client ... and communicating your motor fuel prices to those dealers. It is clear you are attempting to induce our client's dealers to breach their contract with our client. Our client reserves the right to issue proceedings against your company without further notice.

They may have reserved the right to issue proceedings, but that is all they did. In fact, one multinational started to offer selected forecourt owners greatly improved deals with prices based on Platts (just like GreatGas) and extra rebates. Generally speaking we ignored our so-called competitors but this irritated us so much that we wrote (by no means for the first time) to the Competition Authority and complained about predatory pricing. The Competition Authority spent nearly three months reviewing our case before deciding that we had no case.

As I have already explained, another thing our competitors did was spread lies about our reliability, prices and service. Of course, forecourt owners would, when talking to Ray, make reference to what they had been told by third parties, but by and large they were unwilling to be quoted. Nevertheless, from time to time, we would catch someone out – usually an area representative – and write to the company they worked for. Sometimes sales representatives would say something directly to us. Either way, the companies were always quick to back down, as this quote from a letter sent to me by one large oil company demonstrates:

> I wish to refer specifically to the allegation of defamation uttered by or on behalf of the company as suggested by you. Anything that may have been said to you and perceived as defamatory was not intended and we apologise if you have taken offence. You will appreciate that we must deny any defamatory remarks were made.

It was gratifying that we had some of the industry rattled. In some respects it was helpful, too, that we were so obviously a topic of conversation on the forecourts of Ireland. There was a downside, though. If we knew a forecourt owner had been given misinformation about us we could do our best to correct it, but what about all the other times we never heard about? In order to counter the growing number of attacks being made against us, we increased our own communication efforts. We had always been diligent about getting our message out there, of course, but in 2008 it became more urgent. If we didn't correct what was being said about us, it could well affect our future plans. For the first time we appointed a PR adviser and received great support from Breda Brown in Unique Media.

In the first ever GreatGas mailing, the one that I sent out when the whole company was no more than a twinkle in my eye, I told the recipients that it would be their only chance to join and that I wouldn't contact them again. At the time I fully intended to live up to that promise, but once GreatGas had been launched it became clear that I would have to go back on it. After trial and error we found that sending a newsletter was the best possible way to reach our targets. I have always felt that printed (rather than electronic) newsletters are a much underutilised tool. A well-presented newsletter will usually be perceived by its recipients in a very positive light: a source of information rather than a sales device. Something that comes through the post, especially now that email is so popular, receives more attention than one might expect. By focusing on case histories and testimonials our regular newsletters did much to wrong-foot our detractors, as well as to generate leads.

We also had our successes in the media. No one could claim that we were operating in a glamorous sector, but even so we managed to get a surprising amount of national coverage. One way we achieved this was by turning a perfectly ordinary story into a snappy headline. No newspaper, for example, would have been interested in the fact that we had signed up six new members, but when Unique Media issued a press release in the summer of 2008 stating that we had signed a €15 million deal, several editors picked up on the story: 'GreatGas gathers steam', trumpeted the *Irish Times*; 'GreatGas sign up €15 million deals', said the *Evening Echo*; while the *Sunday Business Post* announced (more sedately), 'GreatGas adds to national network'. Better still, the media made much of the fact that we 'had increased fuel sales by as much as 195 per cent' for our members (*Evening Echo*) and helped them 'boost retail sales by an average of 22 per cent' (*Irish Times*). Although we never promoted ourselves as the consumer's friend, the media picked up on this also. Lower wholesale prices meant more competitive pump prices.

I wish I could say that the positive press coverage provided the necessary reassurance that we were a solid business to either ConocoPhillips or our bankers. One or other could very easily have put us out of business during our third year of trading. It was, to say the least, frustrating. By the middle of 2008 we were funding the signage changes for new members at the rate of one a month and still had positive cash flow. We paid our bills on time and we had excellent security in the form of bank guarantees. I had also provided our bank with an increased personal guarantee of €1 million. Despite these positive signs, ConocoPhillips was forever threatening to cut off our supply without faster payment and bigger guarantees and the bank refused all my appeals to provide additional finance. Profit, as I had learned in my early banking days, is not the same as cash.

There was another serious financial issue during 2008: the price of oil. In 2005 oil was on average $50.04 a barrel. In 2006 this figure rose to $58.30 a barrel. Then in 2007 it went up to $64.20 a barrel. That's a pretty big hike over the space of two years but it was nothing compared to what happened in 2008, when the average price spiralled to a record $91.48. This was the *average* price – the highest barrel price was an eye-watering $147 in July 2008. Many consumers are under the misapprehension that oil companies like to see prices rise, as it allows them to widen their margins. In fact, what actually happens is that demand falls and margins are squeezed. So although our turnover was rising it was because we were signing up new members. Consumers, having seen petrol prices double in a short space of time, were being very careful about how often they used their vehicles, and the same was even more true of commercial road users. In the latter half of 2008 prices began to fall again and in 2009 the average barrel price was back to $53.48. I think it is fair to say that Ray and I breathed a long sigh of relief when things began to return to normal.

13

2008: The Year of Living Dangerously

From the moment it launched, GreatGas was always something of a rollercoaster ride, but never more so than in 2008. I can't better express how fraught it was than to say that in the first half of the year I barely took a single day off, not even at weekends. Of course, this was by no means entirely due to GreatGas. Many of my other projects demanded attention during that period. In particular, two of my start-ups, My Tradesman and Kendlebell, although not quite on life support, were both looking decidedly unwell. The world economy had begun its slowdown and it was widely recognised that Ireland was heading towards recession. Property prices were falling, consumer confidence was falling, unemployment was starting to rise and the banks had tightened their lending criteria.

Against this background, I had to find extra cash to fund GreatGas's expansion. I decided in January that I would take a new tack. Instead of looking for a single venture capitalist willing to invest €250,000, I would try to raise €970,000 in new equity by placing 4,850,000 ordinary shares at €0.20 each. With this in mind I created an information memorandum in which I explained the history of the business and its current trading position. The purpose of the fundraising was summarised as follows:

- To pay for new sales staff to speed up the conversion of prospects to members

- To meet the cost of rebranding our new members' forecourts at an average price of €25,000 each
- To reduce our bank debt (we had a term loan of €400,000 in place)
- To fund increased trading – as we grew, we needed cash to bridge the gap between paying our suppliers and receiving funds from our customers
- To facilitate a credit insurance bond for our suppliers

Most investors want to know when they are going to get their money back. In the memorandum I anticipated that a trade sale would probably occur in 2012 and suggested that even before then there could be a dividend flow. All in all, if I say so myself, it was an impressive document, packed with relevant data and describing a growing company that would expand even faster with a relatively modest amount of additional capital in place. My conservative projections (and bear in mind that I was a banker for many years and tend to take a gloomy view of business forecasts) showed that turnover in 2009 should hit €109 million with €568,000 of profit and that within three years it was not unreasonable to predict profits of €1.4 million.

The document was well received. I made presentations to a number of fund managers, private investors and potential business partners and – without exception – everyone agreed that GreatGas was an interesting company. What no one was willing to do, however, was subscribe for the shares. In May, after lengthy negotiation, I signed a new, higher personal guarantee to the bank, allowing us to slightly up the pace of our expansion. A few days later I sent a memo to my fellow directors in which I stated that, 'Hopefully this will keep ConocoPhillips quiet for a while.' In that memo I went on to say:

> At this stage I think the possibility of a white knight taking a stake and investing €1 million in GreatGas is no longer realistic and something I would now only wish to entertain as an absolute last resort. I now see GreatGas as a very long-term investment, which must be developed to maximise income for the shareholders.

In other words, a major change of direction. We must accept the situation for what it was. There would be no accelerated expansion. Instead of ploughing every penny of cash we could lay our hands on into the business, we should start thinking about paying ourselves a dividend. It was, in a sense, an admission of defeat, but it was imperative as personal cash flow was tightening due to the economic collapse that was unfolding all around us.

Frustrated, I turned to my other projects and even contemplated some new ventures. I had heard a rumour that one of the Dublin radio stations could be up for sale and, having invested in radio before (and having come out well ahead), I was keen to explore the possibilities. Indeed, I was so busy that when Gerry Wilson from Emo Oil telephoned in June to suggest we get together for an informal chat, I was not able to meet him until August.

When I was new to business, and less experienced, I used to get excited by calls like Gerry's. The mildest of enquiries by the representative of a larger venture would set my imagination alight. I would see myself selling out for a vast sum and perhaps being given a new, highly lucrative role in the merged organisation. Gradually I came to learn that big companies routinely explore the potential acquisition of smaller competitors. It is an excellent way for them to learn about what is happening in the market and, of course, a lean, rapidly growing business often has much to teach a lumbering commercial colossus. I had had my expectations raised, my hopes dashed and my brains picked before. So, although I was intrigued to hear from Gerry, I made no assumptions about the outcome of any meeting.

Still, I won't deny that as I was driving to Portlaoise, which is where Gerry had his office, I allowed myself to hope that Emo Oil, part of DCC Energy, itself a subsidiary of DCC plc, a multinational group based in Dublin, might be interested in investing in GreatGas. I was encouraged by the fact that, unlike most of our competitors, Emo Oil had always appeared to be indifferent to GreatGas. There was no evidence that they had tried to undermine our position with forecourt owners and thus there was no ill will to overcome before we could hold a meaningful conversation. Indeed, we had a good meeting; I asked Gerry if he and DCC Energy's managing director, Donal Murphy, would visit the GreatGas offices in Churchtown to explore opportunities between us.

By August 2008 I had given the GreatGas pitch a hundred times. I had given it to forecourt owners, recruits, employees, bankers, investors, venture capitalists, accountants, business angels, journalists, suppliers, competitors, lawyers, friends, relations and random strangers who had asked me what I did for a living. Knowing that the best presentations incorporate props, I didn't just tell, I frequently showed, by using photographs, models and merchandise to illustrate various points. I had even placed it within the context of Churchtown and its renewal. You might think, especially as GreatGas was just one of dozens of projects I was interested in, that I might be somewhat blasé every time I came to speak about it. Not so. Whenever I stood up and uttered the words, 'Let me just explain what makes GreatGas so special …' I fell in love with the concept and the company all over again.

Although only weeks earlier I had rejected the idea of selling a stake in GreatGas, it would be dishonest of me not to admit that it was my intention to try to persuade DCC Energy to take a one-third stake in the company. I didn't have a price in mind but felt that in principle it was a deal that would work out for everyone. GreatGas would get the cash it needed to expand; I would still have a substantial equity interest and the motivation to build the company into the national group I believed it could be; and DCC would increase their share of the Irish market. When I suggested the one-third option to Donal Murphy, however, he dismissed the idea with a breezy wave of his hand. 'If we are going to do any sort of a deal', he said, 'it will be a complete buyout. We're interested in all of GreatGas or nothing.' All or nothing? It hadn't ever been my intention to sell out completely, but as he spoke the words I found to my surprise that I was not entirely opposed to the idea. After a moment's hesitation I agreed to exploratory talks.

Exploratory talks. The term has an optimistic sound to it, hinting at high-powered discussions between top executives in elegant settings. It hints at quiet negotiation, eventual agreement, an exchange of contracts and an impressive signing session (perhaps discreetly photographed) followed by a celebratory bottle of champagne. The reality is generally more ordinary. In fact, looking back on all the various sales I have been involved with, the process has never once been even remotely glamorous. It must also be said that many proposed sales never actually take place. Just because one is talking doesn't mean that anything will happen. Indeed, I didn't – in my heart of hearts – expect the DCC Energy deal to come off. Why not? Early on it was clear that we had very different ideas about what GreatGas was worth. Donal Murphy, naturally enough, wanted a bargain. Possibly he may have thought that I needed the money more than I did, which was probably true. At any rate his initial offer was so low that I couldn't see us ever reaching mutually acceptable terms.

14

THE NIGHT OF THE OILMAN'S BALL

Most corporate sales – especially to a publicly quoted company – follow a set pattern. To begin with it is usual for the vendor to appoint both a firm of accountants and a firm of lawyers to represent them. We appointed the accountancy firm BDO to act as advisers, but as I had always personally handled the legal needs of GreatGas I refrained from appointing a firm of lawyers until the last moment, when I appointed O'Shea Barry Solicitors. As I have already mentioned, I wasn't totally convinced our deal would ever get to the stage where we would require one. It is usual for purchasers to sign a non-disclosure agreement before the vendor supplies any sensitive facts and figures. This, in theory, stops the purchaser from passing all the information given to them to third parties. As we didn't have a firm of lawyers I adapted an agreement I had used before. It opened with the words:

> Whereas GreatGas Petroleum plc (GGP) has agreed that it shall disclose to DCC Energy (DCC) certain confidential information for the purpose of DCC evaluating the prospect of an acquisition or investment in GGP ...

In my experience such agreements are mostly pointless. People are, by and large, trustworthy and I certainly wouldn't disclose any sensitive information to a company I thought was likely to broadcast it.

Anyway, even if one can prove that someone has been indiscreet, to prosecute with any degree of success one would have to show that this had resulted in financial loss. Such a thing isn't easy to prove and, of course, the legal costs associated with pursuing this type of case are prohibitive. Still, it is traditional to put such an agreement in place, and who was I to turn my back on tradition? I sent off the agreement to DCC Energy on 7 August 2008 and it says everything about the progress being made that it was several weeks before they returned it.

Indeed, you will get a feel for how little I expected to strike a deal with DCC Energy from what happened at the GreatGas September board meeting. The possibility of a sale was still low down on the agenda, as you will see from this summary of the meeting:

1. We approved the minutes from previous meeting.
2. I made a few general remarks about how solid the business was and we all tried not to look too smug when I predicted the profits for the current and future years.
3. There was a detailed review of the year to date, followed by a discussion of the current challenges and the need for increased bank guarantees.
4. Ray provided an update on trading conditions, oil prices, foreign currency considerations, our existing member/customer relations and current sales prospects, bearing in mind that we were not trying to expand as rapidly as we once had.
5. We engaged in a detailed discussion of the ConocoPhillips demands and how we were going to meet them.
6. I explained that DCC Energy were interested in buying us out but that so far not much had happened.
7. We approved the 2007 accounts.
8. We set the date for the next meeting.
9. We decided that there was no other business.

The subject that really dominated the meeting was how we were going to put sufficient financial security in place to satisfy ConocoPhillips. In late August they had written to us demanding new, substantially higher guarantees, and in a follow-up telephone conversation had made it clear that they were not open to negotiation. We were, they instructed, to increase our bank guarantee to €2 million (almost double what we already had in place) immediately and the amount was to rise in incremental stages to €4 million within three years. If we failed in this we could expect them to stop supplying us. We didn't commit either way during the call, but inwardly I was very worried. It had only been three months since the existing guarantee had been put in place. I wondered why they felt the need to look for extra security again so soon. Could it be that we were still growing too quickly for their liking? (Despite our best efforts to slow our expansion, sales were still rising every month.) It occurred to me that it might just be in the nature of the ConocoPhillips finance team to push. We had (eventually) met their last demands, so perhaps it was simply that they thought they would ask for more to see what would happen. There was, incidentally, a strange disconnect between ConocoPhillips' local management, which was supportive, and their financial team, based in Wales, which was hard on us. Anyway, it didn't matter why they were laying down these extra conditions. The key point was that we had to decide what to do.

Although we always took ConocoPhillips' demands (and there were plenty of them) seriously, we never lost sight of the fact that we were good customers and had never once failed to pay on time. Nevertheless, it was clear we would have to try to meet their demands. It was too early to rely on DCC Energy so I cast around for other solutions. My initial action was to draw up a list of friends and associates who might, at a price, be willing to help underwrite our bank guarantees. A year later it would have been a list of zero as by then the Irish economy had completely collapsed and everyone I might have asked had other priorities. In September 2008, however, the impact of the crash was several months away, and I did manage to find one such individual and was actually negotiating with him at the time of the board meeting.

Another option that I decided to pursue was invoice discounting, or factoring. This is a way of raising money on the back of your debtors. In essence a company gives a financial institution – often a bank subsidiary – security in the form of the invoices it has issued, and in exchange it can borrow a percentage of what it is owed. For instance, if GreatGas issued invoices of, say, €100,000 the bank might, the same day, lend

€80,000. This wasn't exactly what we required, but I thought the fact that we were on course for over €100 million turnover in 2009 and could offer such excellent security might appeal to one or two of the invoice-discounting firms. In the event, it only appealed to one, Lloyds TSB, and we put in a formal application on 4 October.

So by mid-October the state of play at GreatGas was as follows: Business was never stronger, with growing sales and no shortage of prospective members and customers keen to buy from us. The ConocoPhillips finance team was bombarding us with letters, emails and faxes containing dark threats about the consequences of failing to get the €2 million guarantee in place. The ConocoPhillips local management team was running with the hares and hunting with the hounds – in other words making supportive noises, but of no practical use. I was trying to persuade at least one friend to help as guarantor. We were waiting to hear what Lloyds TSB would say with regard to invoice discounting. The DCC Energy deal was still a possibility, but progress was slow. We had supplied them with our financial data and had had a meeting in Dublin at which their proposed valuation had fallen so short of my own I did half wonder if it was worth pursuing.

Then, the week of 21 October, things started to fall apart and come together all at the same time. The bad news was that we had a conversation with ConocoPhillips that made it clear we were running out of time; the friend who had agreed to provide the guarantee finally said he was no longer in a position to help; and Lloyds TSB declined our application for invoice discounting. The good news was that the GreatGas and DCC teams, together with all the legal and corporate finance advisers, had had yet another meeting and at the end of it Donal and I had shaken hands on a deal that worked well for all concerned.

A handshake isn't a contract, of course, and it certainly isn't money in the bank. But it is a move in the right direction. DCC Energy's initial offer had been based on historical profits, our balance sheet and turnover more than on future potential. What we had ended up agreeing was something altogether different: the shareholders in GreatGas would be paid for their shares over a much longer period and the payment would be linked to the ongoing profitability of the company. Moreover, instead of simply absorbing GreatGas into the Emo network, it would remain a separate, stand-alone brand. This was, of course, much more of a gamble for the GreatGas shareholders. If the company's profits for the next few years were disappointing, we wouldn't, bluntly, have much to look forward to despite all our effort. On the other hand, if the company experienced the level of growth we all anticipated, our gains would be considerably higher than we had ever imagined. Moreover, DCC Energy was happy to leave the day-to-day management with Ray and to leave me as non-executive chairman. The offices would remain in Churchtown, too, which I liked because it was both convenient and beneficial to the local economy. On 29 October, with the earn-out strategy agreed, DCC Energy started the due diligence process.

If the first stage to any corporate sale is usually the signing of a non-disclosure agreement, the second is due diligence. This is an exceedingly tedious procedure for all involved because it requires the vendor to supply vast quantities of information to the potential purchaser. Some of the information is easy to get one's hands on – 'a certified copy of the certificate of incorporation', for instance, or 'the names of all the officers of the company including the full names of each director and the secretary'. Other information, such as 'copies of all the company's tax returns' and 'a list of all the company's tangible assets together with audited book value' takes a little searching for. DCC Energy sent us eleven closely typed pages of requests and I don't think it is an exaggeration to say that Ray, Michelle and I devoted hours of our time every day to finding the relevant documentation. During this process the negotiation continued. Crucially, it was agreed that the bulk of the purchase price would be based on the profitability of the company several years ahead – 2011, 2012, 2013 and 2014. Given that we hoped to close the sale in 2008, that meant that my fellow shareholders and I were gambling on a very rosy future.

On 5 November we had a somewhat unusual meeting with DCC Energy at the Shelbourne Hotel in Dublin. It was the night of the Oilman's Ball – dinner really – and the one night of the year when the entire industry gathers together for a social occasion organised by the Irish Petroleum Industry Association. Close observers might have noticed four gentlemen in evening wear – Donal, Gerry, Ray and myself – having an intense conversation in one of the quieter corridors. We were ironing out the details. A couple of weeks later, on 25 November, DCC Energy's lawyers sent us a 'heads of agreement' document. This was a plain English version of the deal we had struck and though clearly marked, in bold capital letters, 'SUBJECT TO CONTRACT', it was the first time I really felt a sale might take place.

That heads of agreement document contained a clause worthy of special note. It was clause 10 and it stated:

> From the date of signing of this memorandum until 31st January 2009, Gerry Murphy (GM) and Ray O'Sullivan (ROS) individually or collectively will not solicit proposals from, or engage in discussions with, other parties to dispose of any of the assets (other than in the ordinary course of business) or share capital of GreatGas. During this period, GM and ROS will cooperate fully with DCC and its representatives to provide all the necessary information and access to enable it to complete its due diligence in an expeditious manner. The parties will make every effort to ensure that the transaction is completed by 20th December 2008.

The parties did make every effort to ensure that the transaction was completed by 20 December 2008, but they failed. And that failure led to a rather serious problem.

15

WHERE EXACTLY ARE THE CAVALRY?

C hristmas Day found my wife, Dorothy, our daughters and me at home in Dublin. I joined the family for dinner, but I didn't participate in all the other celebrations. There was no watching a film, visiting neighbours, sitting in front of the fire with a drink or snoozing in an armchair for me. For much of the day – indeed, for much of the holiday period – I was to be found in my study with a piece of work that had been absorbing most of my waking hours for the previous fortnight. I was trying to identify, find, order and, where necessary, replace every single one of the official company documents relating to GreatGas.

I was performing what was proving to be an extremely laborious task because, as Gustav Mahler so wisely pointed out, 'All that is not perfect down to the smallest detail is doomed to perish.' Without the correct paperwork the deal with DCC Energy was at risk of being called off or postponed for an indefinite period. Either would have been potentially calamitous for GreatGas since, at the beginning of December, ConocoPhillips had made it clear that we were perilously close to having our supplies cut off. We had won a stay of execution by telling them about the DCC Energy deal, which would, obviously, put us on a completely different financial footing. With considerable reluctance they had agreed to continue supplying our members and customers until the day specified in the heads of agreement we had signed with DCC Energy.

Even as our contact in the ConocoPhillips' finance department uttered the words, 'Okay, we'll give you until the twentieth of December', I knew I had another serious problem to deal with. Back in 2005, aware that we might want to sell GreatGas to a third party, I had appointed a firm that specialised in company secretarial work to look after all the official documentation. All the relevant paperwork, from board minutes to cancelled share certificates and from resolutions appointing directors to copies of guarantees, had been sent to this firm. Every year they had invoiced us for their services and whenever I paid their bill I congratulated myself on having had the foresight to get a firm of experts involved. Ha! When I asked for all the GreatGas records to be returned in anticipation of completing the sale to DCC Energy, I received an appalling shock: not only had the firm failed to do the required work, they had actually managed to lose some of the files. Not surprisingly, DCC Energy's legal advisers would not buy a company that couldn't even produce an up-to-date register of shareholders.

You may be wondering, incidentally, what it was that made the paperwork so difficult to complete. GreatGas, being a sort of hybrid co-operative, had 47 different shareholders. Of these, 38 held less than 1 per cent each, representing just 12.2 per cent of the company. By right, these minority shareholders, largely GreatGas forecourt owners, had to receive full information about the DCC Energy offer and an explanation of what it meant to them. Then, provided they were happy to sell their shares, they had to sign the appropriate stock transfer form and return their share certificates. If any one of them had refused to do so it would have meant delaying the sale by several weeks. I wrote to them all on 30 December and almost immediately afterwards Ray started making contact with them one by one to check they were happy to proceed. As it happens they all were, but I won't pretend that the whole process didn't add to the tension.

One of the things I liked and admired about the way Donal behaved when we were negotiating the GreatGas deal is that he thought long term. He couldn't have failed to know that we were vulnerable. He had seen our accounts, bank statements and guarantees. He had probably spoken to his own contacts at ConocoPhillips, too, about how things stood between us. He could have taken advantage of this situation by delaying the deal in order to better the terms, knowing that we were caught between a rock and a hard place. Nothing like that happened. Nevertheless, I was conscious as I worked through Christmas and the New Year that if the sale of GreatGas didn't close quickly we were at risk of losing everything.

During my 25 years in banking, I obtained some hands-on experience of managing crises. I discovered that no matter how much advance planning you do nothing prepares you for disaster when it strikes. This is partly because catastrophes are rarely the ones you anticipate and partly because events can unfold with unexpected speed and intensity. I was absolutely certain that if ConocoPhillips stopped supplying GreatGas with fuel it would spell potential ruin. The moment a couple of anticipated deliveries failed to arrive the word would get out. Every driver knows what happens to petrol stations with empty tanks. You stop visiting them. The forecourt owners know this, too. If GreatGas didn't supply the fuel that had been ordered we could expect our members and customers to order elsewhere. The media would quickly get to hear about it. No amount of crisis management would save the day. Business would, literally, dry up. On Monday 5 January, the first working day of the New Year, I couriered all the completed records to DCC Energy's lawyers in Dublin. The only outstanding paperwork was the stock transfer forms and the share certificates. A tentative date for completion was fixed: Monday 19 January. We had to keep ConocoPhillips from taking action for two weeks.

Anyway, we did everything we could think of to try to prevent ConocoPhillips from effectively pulling the plug. I did not waste my efforts on any sort of long-term plan. If the DCC Energy deal failed, there would be no time to find another source of finance. However, I tried the banks, again, and also various personal contacts to see whether they could help out on a temporary basis, but in the new economic climate the answer was a universal 'no'. I had, of course, already lent GreatGas all the money I could lay my hands on, and more besides. Other actions I contemplated included asking DCC Energy for a short-term loan and selling off, at high speed, one of my other assets – perhaps a property. I was worried that the former would result in further delay and perhaps a renegotiation of our deal, and I couldn't actually think how to achieve the latter. I wasn't in a panic – I wasn't even losing sleep – but I did experience a constant sense of foreboding as I waited, impatiently, for Monday 19 January. When I awoke on Friday 16 I heaved a huge sigh of relief. Only one day to go and then we would be out of the woods. I had my breakfast as usual, made a few telephone calls and was just heading off to a meeting when Ray called.

'Have you checked your email?'

'No.'

'I think you'd better.'

'ConocoPhillips?'

'Yes.'

The email was every bit as bad as I had anticipated:

As I am sure you are aware your current usage is excessive against the security we hold. We are taking payments early in an attempt to maintain the limit and supply. However, each payment is two days from hitting the banking system and as I have previously explained we are a further five working days from being confirmed that the payments will not be recalled.

The current total of payments in the system that we are not able to consider as cleared is a staggering €1,440,494.66. When you add to this the items on the account we have an exposure of €1,845,978.36 which does not include any lifts from yesterday evening onwards.

We need to reduce this figure. The biggest chunk of the exposure is due to the vagaries of the DD system and I therefore propose that we cease this activity.

We need from you a TT payment [bank transfer] of €400,000 in our bank each Monday ... starting on the 19th January 2009 and during the week ... will contact you regarding how much extra we'll need prior to the next Monday's payment.

Items on your account will be called forward for collection and your supply from Monday will be dependent on the aforementioned €400,000 being received.

Given that we were only a working day away from closing our deal, it seemed particularly unreasonable of ConocoPhillips to threaten us in this way. True, the threat was coming from one of their overseas credit analysts rather than a member of their local management but still, it was aggressive bearing in mind we had never missed a payment. The question was what we should do about it. One option was to take no action whatsoever. On Monday morning, when ConocoPhillips checked their bank account and found that the €400,000 hadn't been credited, their first action would be to call the GreatGas office in Churchtown. As Ray and I would be at DCC Energy's lawyers signing the sale and purchase contract, warranties and other paperwork there would be no one they could really talk to. Even if they cancelled Monday's deliveries then and there, by early afternoon we would be able to forward them hard evidence that GreatGas was now owned by DCC Energy. This would, surely, be sufficient to get the supplies flowing again and, if it didn't, well, it would be in the new owner's interest to lend GreatGas the necessary cash. The other option was to contact Donal at DCC Energy and explain the position. This was clearly the ethical thing to do. With all the resources at his disposal there was no doubt that he would be able to satisfy ConocoPhillips' desire for extra security. It had the added advantage of putting ConocoPhillips on the spot. If they wanted to retain GreatGas as a customer after the deal went through, they would need to appease DCC Energy. The risk was that Donal would take some unforeseen action. I couldn't completely get it out of my head that his response might, in some way, result in the DCC Energy acquisition of GreatGas coming to nought.

16

WHEN YOU DON'T KNOW WHAT TO DO, DO NOTHING

We didn't (because we couldn't) transfer the €400,000 ConocoPhillips had demanded into their account on Monday 19 January. We didn't call them with an explanation, either. At 9 a.m., Ray, our legal adviser and I were shown into a meeting room in the offices of the legal firm DCC Energy had appointed to handle the GreatGas acquisition. We had with us two large boxes containing all the share certificates, share transfer forms and other paperwork we would be required to furnish before the agreement could be completed. As we were setting everything out on the table the DCC Energy team joined us, followed by two lawyers and their clerks. The clerks hurried in and out carrying piles of bound documents. Each binder bristled with little sticky coloured markers indicating where signatures would be required. At 9.30 we began.

It took over three hours. Every piece of paper had to be read and reread and, in many cases, signed by four people. Each signature then had to be witnessed. Finally, as lunchtime approached, one of the lawyers passed a thick bundle of cheques across the table to me – one for each of the shareholders. While Ray was checking the amounts and names, I slipped out to send a fax I had actually written up earlier. It was to ConocoPhillips and in it I explained that GreatGas was now part of DCC Energy, the largest distributor of fuel in Britain and Ireland. I apologised for not making the transfer as requested but pointed out that now the sale had been completed we wished to take advantage of the new terms that had been promised.

It has always been my philosophy, when I am not sure what I should do, to do nothing. I call this philosophy 'management by ignorance'. Put simply, ignore it until you know what to do. On Friday, after receiving the ConocoPhillips email demanding the €400,000 transfer, my strategy had been one of masterful inaction. We didn't contact ConocoPhillips and we didn't contact DCC Energy. Over the weekend I did think about the situation fairly frequently – I would defy anyone in my position not to – but I pride myself on the fact that I didn't mention it once to my family or the friends with whom we had dinner on that Saturday night. Whether ConocoPhillips had intended to carry out their threat to disrupt our supplies I couldn't say. If they had, they must have changed their mind because when, after a quick celebratory lunch, I called the GreatGas office in Churchtown there was no news.

My emotions about the sale were somewhat mixed. I was, naturally, delighted to be banking a substantial cheque and was looking forward with eager anticipation to further, hopefully even larger, cheques in the years to come. I felt deeply relieved, too, that I would no longer be scrabbling around looking for cash to keep GreatGas going. There was more stress involved in that than I had admitted at the time. Most of all, however, I felt a glow of satisfaction with regard to the agreement itself. For me the sale was a beginning, not an end. How much the shareholders, including myself, would ultimately receive depended on future profitability. Future profitability depended, in part, on how well we performed. My mind was awhirl with plans for the company's expansion.

If this book were about the GreatGas story, and not about how I became an accidental entrepreneur, there would now follow several chapters about that expansion. As it is, I will simply summarise.

Immediately after the sale, thanks to the new terms of trade, the GreatGas bank account became flush with cash. To the best of my recollection, within three weeks of the deal we were sitting on a balance of several million euros. More importantly, for the first time we had sufficient resources to fund our growth. Thanks to our improved buying power since we sold, GreatGas's members and customers have enjoyed consistently low fuel prices – a benefit many have passed on to their customers. Everyone, as it were, has been a winner. On the cover of this book I boasted (regrettably there is no other word to describe it) that we turned €3,749 into a €100 million company in just three years. In fact, I exaggerated very slightly. We started the company in 2005, Ray signed up the first GreatGas member in April 2006 and we didn't actually hit the €100 million annualised turnover figure until 2009. I would like to pretend that I feel guilty about misleading you, but I don't. It makes a very good and arresting headline.

I have deliberately not mentioned how much money we earned from the sale of GreatGas. My concern is that, if I publish the figure, some people will feel I am showing off, others that I am making a fuss about nothing. I will only say that it was a considerable amount of money to us. In different circumstances I could, in fact, have retired very comfortably on it if I had been so minded. Instead I am still working, and working as hard, because when the Irish economy collapsed in 2009 many of the small and medium-sized businesses I was involved in were badly affected and required investment.

You may be wondering if, given that my business career has been punctuated with ups and downs, I regret any of the choices I have made. Not a day passes without me thinking I could have done something better, but equally I have come to realise that it doesn't in the grand scheme of things really matter, and there is little if any benefit in spending too much time looking in the rear-view mirror. What's important to me is to feel that I am doing something moderately useful, meeting a need, creating employment, learning from my mistakes and making a contribution to society.

As you can't have failed to notice, there is a random quality to my choice of business ventures. In 1971 George Cockcroft, an academic, published a book called *The Dice Man* under the name Luke Rhinehart, in which the main character makes all his decisions based on the throw of a dice. My own business decisions are not quite as casual or arbitrary but I do hate the idea of too much business planning. I have found that it is much better and more enjoyable to be an accidental entrepreneur. I hope you'll join me.

17

Epilogue

GreatGas became part of the DCC Energy division in January 2009 and I continued as chairman until I retired in November 2012, having successfully completed the agreed earn-out. The economic climate in Ireland in which GreatGas operated from 2009 onwards was very challenging but, despite this headwind, GreatGas continued to grow as part of DCC.

For me, the DCC deal was a lifesaver; with the understanding of my banks and support from friends, family and colleagues, I was able to navigate my other investments through the worst economic downturn since the Great Depression. To these institutions and people I am most grateful.

Ray O'Sullivan continues as managing director of GreatGas but now with a greater role within the larger DCC Energy division. In July 2014, GreatGas moved from the Market House in Churchtown and was centralised in Portlaoise within the DCC Energy division as part of the company's restructuring within Ireland. This was a very understandable move by DCC, but a sad day for the staff in Churchtown who had helped create the business, and for me too.

Since I left home in 1972 to make my way in the world, I have followed a long, winding and wonderful road. In 2010 accidental entrepreneurship took me overseas, first to London and more recently to Abu Dhabi. Working outside Ireland has been good to me, but if I had to predict the future I would say that I will soon be back again in Churchtown focusing on community projects.

Abu Dhabi, September 2014

PART II

How to Start a Successful Business with Hardly any Money (Even in a Recession)

18

WHY YOU SHOULD READ ON

Have you thought that it would be nice to have your own business, but been put off by the effort, risk and money required? Are you determined to start something, but not quite sure how to overcome all the obstacles in your way? Do you actually own a business, but feel that it isn't reaching its full potential? Part II of this book is for you.

My premise is simple: I want to pass on the lessons I have learned launching and running small to medium-sized businesses. It is, unashamedly, a sort of pick and mix of information, ideas, tips, strategy, tactics, philosophy and encouragement. If I had to sum it up, I would say it contains everything I wish I had known when I was getting going. Its purpose is to save you time, worry and cash as well as – crucially – to maximise your chances of success.

I hope you will find what I have to say inspirational. This book is written in plain English (the only sort of English I like to write) but I have tried to imbue it with some of the excitement and pleasure I have had from being an entrepreneur. Whether you dabble in commerce (maybe doing something part-time) or throw yourself in at the deep end, if you do it right it is great fun and very, very satisfying.

What I can definitely promise is that you will find this section of the book practical. Theory is all very well, but when you're trying to get a venture off the ground you don't want to read about the trials and tribulations faced by the chief executive of some massive multi-national. You want hands-on advice from someone who has done it.

My Credentials

Business books tend to be written by (a) academics, (b) self-help gurus or (c) indescribably rich people who have made a fortune doing one thing really well.

Fine. They all have something to contribute. But to my mind many of them are not in the real world. My book is based on my personal experience of launching and starting a string of small businesses. I'm not (a) in an ivory tower, (b) trying to get to you to attend a seminar or (c) so wealthy that I have forgotten what it is like to worry about paying the monthly bills.

Moreover, I am not trying to hide the truth. My business career has been messy. I have had some dismal failures and I am not afraid to talk about them or where I went wrong so that you can avoid doing the same. Equally, I have had some successes and I am more than happy to explain why (and to admit it when it was pure luck).

Will you be hearing how to make a go of it from someone who is successful? That depends on how you measure success. If pressed as to how much money I have made, my answer would be the same as the actor Walter Matthau after he had a suspected heart attack on the set of *Buddy Buddy*. His co-star Jack Lemmon rushed over, put a cushion under his head and asked, 'Are you comfortable?' Matthau replied, 'I make a living.' More importantly, so far as I'm concerned, is the fact that I am earning my living doing something I love. I feel challenged and fulfilled. I have created employment and made a contribution to society.

Exploding Myths

I am looking forward to exploding a number of myths in this book. The first is that you need lots of capital to start a business. You don't. The second is that business is risky. It needn't be. And the third is that you must commit 100 per cent to make a business work. Total nonsense.

The State of the Economy Makes No Difference

I believe that it is easier to start a business during a recession than during a boom. Moreover, such businesses tend to be stronger and more successful in the long term. I am going to prove it, too. Anyway, another vital subject raised in this book is how to make a downturn in the economy work for you.

Why 'Accidental'?

The last thing I ever thought I would be is an entrepreneur. There is nothing entrepreneurial about my background. I come from a conservative farming family and after leaving school I spent 25 years in banking (this was before the banking sector ran into the sand) and had actually planned to stick it out in banking until retirement.

Then, entirely by accident, I started a small business. Nothing fancy, just a holiday hostel in a rural, out-of-the-way location. Later on, I thought it would be nice to be able to offer guests a drink and something to eat, so I opened a bar and restaurant. One thing led to another and somehow – even now I am at a loss to explain it – I ended up launching (or helping to launch) rather a lot of other businesses, including a property company, a football-themed café, a medical clinic and an oil distribution company.

A pretty varied list, but in every case I was actually trying to solve someone else's problem. The holiday hostel, for example, was actually part of a programme to regenerate the village I grew up in. So was the property company. The football-themed café came about because I was trying to work with a friend; the medical clinic was me trying to help out the friend of a friend. And so forth. They were all launched as businesses, of course, but they weren't started solely with profit in mind.

I have discovered that there are some massive benefits to launching a business not as a business per se, but for other, non-financial, reasons. So many benefits, in fact, that I would actually urge anyone thinking of going into business to put the whole money side of the equation to one side and instead think about who it is going to help and how. In doing so you will become an accidental entrepreneur. You won't be alone. Some of the most successful businesses in the world were started this way.

One More Thing ...

I feel it is only fair to warn you that if your sole interest is in making lots of money then you are going to be disappointed with this book. Accidental entrepreneurs are usually not greedy. Some of us are motivated by such things as the desire to support our family, help others, solve problems, be creative or get out of debt; and/or simply by a yearning for independence. Others of us aren't actually that motivated at all. So, if it's entirely about lucre for you, I strongly recommend returning this book to the shop now, before it gets dog-eared and they refuse to take it back. Don't feel bad. (You'll know you're an accidental entrepreneur, incidentally, if you are the sort of person who means to return something to a shop but somehow never gets around to it.)

19

THE WAY OF THE ACCIDENTAL ENTREPRENEUR

I have nearly a thousand business and self-help books in my library, so although what follows is going to sound like a massive generalisation, it is actually based on a lot of reading. Authors of business books frequently seem to come up with a clever-sounding idea. Many of those books, however, fail to live up to the blurb on the jacket and after a couple of chapters disappointment sets in, either because the idea is not great to begin with or because it is easily explained and most of the book is simply padding to justify the cover price. There are notable exceptions, but generally the 'take away' can usually be summed up in a page or two.

Which is why, here and now, I am going to admit that the accidental entrepreneur concept is really only a way to get entrepreneurs and would-be entrepreneurs to look at what they are doing, or want to do, from an entirely different perspective. Once I have explained the idea I am not going to keep banging on about it. My sole purpose is to provide a framework. In particular, I want to encourage you to forget – for the time being – profit, productivity, planning, positive thinking and all the other things that business gurus promote. Instead, open your mind (remembering that I am a former banker not prone to hippy-dippyisms) to chance.

How to Identify an Accidental Entrepreneur

It is often said that entrepreneurs are born, not made. Rubbish. I agree that some people do have entrepreneurship in their genetic make-up or, because of the way they are raised, appear to. From what I have observed, however, this group is actually in the minority. Much more common are people who reach a point in their career path where it becomes logical for them to give up paid employment and branch out on their own. Finally, there is the group who interest me most: entrepreneurs who stumble into it by accident.

What marks us accidental entrepreneurs out is, of course, that we never really intended to launch a business in the first place. I am not saying that we have never thought about it, but only in an idle, speculative way, much as you might consider climbing Mount Everest or visiting the North Pole. Commerce holds no glamour for us and we are, by and large, indifferent to gain. I don't believe that accidental entrepreneurs conform to a personality type but in general I would say that we are self-effacing, modest and disinclined to over-analyse. Obviously, we must have a certain amount of determination or we wouldn't achieve anything. Our primary goal, however, is to solve a problem or meet some need, and ultimately the fact that this involves setting up and managing a business is usually peripheral. Accidental entrepreneurs challenge the idea that business leaders must be focused on gain, growth and efficiency. Instead, we are likely to be concerned, if not obsessed, with achieving a non-business objective.

You Will Find Us Everywhere

Once you start looking for accidental entrepreneurs you will find us everywhere. Famous examples that spring instantly to mind include Anita Roddick (Body Shop); Richard Branson (Virgin); Tony Elliott (*Time Out*); Craig Newmark (Craigslist); Perry Chen, Yancey Strickler and Charles Adler (Kickstarter); Tim Martin (JD Wetherspoon); and James Dyson (Dyson). If I had to pick just one it would be Derek Sivers, who founded a business called CD Baby in 1997. Sivers, a musician, didn't have a record deal so he decided to make his own CDs and sell them online. When he came up with this idea, e-commerce was in its infancy. He built a simple site and sold a few CDs. Musician friends asked Sivers to start selling their CDs for them, so he did. One thing led to another and CD Baby became a massive, multi-million-dollar online business selling independent music. Eventually a giant dotcom came along and acquired the company for $20 million. Sivers went back to his first love, which was being a musician.

It isn't just the fact that Sivers never planned to become an entrepreneur that makes the CD Baby story interesting. He ran his company in an extremely unconventional way. Unlike many other large-scale online retailers, Sivers felt that customers should be able to contact his company by telephone. The phones were always answered within two rings, from 7 a.m. to 10 p.m. seven days a week. If the office lines were engaged, the call would be put through to the warehouse. Sometimes musicians would mess the CD Baby staff around and cause them a lot of extra work. CD Baby never charged for this but instead asked the customer to order them something from the local pizza restaurant. Apparently, pizzas would arrive at the offices on a regular basis. Incidentally, when the company needed new staff Sivers couldn't be bothered to conduct interviews or take up references. Instead he would ask existing members of staff to hire their friends.

Sivers, being an accidental entrepreneur, had no preconceived idea about how things ought to be done, so he simply pleased himself. Another wonderful example of this is Chris Rufer, founder of the Morning Star Company based in California. In 1970 Rufer bought a lorry and started transporting tomatoes from farms to canning factories. As the business grew he decided that he wouldn't appoint any managers. Not one. Now Morning Star has annual revenue of more than $350 million, employs 2,400 people and, interestingly, pays 15 per cent above the US average salary and 35 per cent more in benefits. Everyone has exactly the same status. As a result there are no directives from above, no promotions and no titles. The company practises what it calls 'self-management'. If you need new equipment to do your job, you buy it. If you see a process that would benefit from different skills, you hire someone. Even the salaries are set by the employees. It shouldn't work, but it does.

I am also impressed with Tim Martin, who founded the pub chain JD Wetherspoon by accident in 1979 and now has over 33,000 staff and a chain of 900 pubs in Britain and Ireland, including one in Blackrock (my favourite suburb in Dublin). Tim says that wealth is not an end in itself, which I also believe is a key philosophy of successful accidental entrepreneurs.

There is one other accidental entrepreneur I want to mention at this point: John Paul DeJoria. In the 1980s he invented a range of shampoos and conditioners and, with his co-founder Paul Mitchell, he began selling them to hairdressers near where he lived in Los Angeles. That range, known as Paul Mitchell, is now sold in more than eighty countries and turns over an estimated $1 billion a year. What makes DeJoria an accidental entrepreneur is the fact that he only started the business because he needed a job. DeJoria has since expanded into all sorts of other completely different areas including tequila, pet care, cyber security and jewellery. He runs his $4 billion empire from a home office without a computer. Instead, if his company presidents (who he says are much smarter than he is) want to get in touch they must call or fax him. I particularly like his attitude to commerce: 'Let it happen. Sometimes people spend too much time thinking. If you just let things happen, the universe works.' This ties in completely with my own philosophy.

Applying the Rules

Successful entrepreneurs who never intended to start a business and/ or who run their businesses in an unorthodox way fly in the face of most of what the so-called management experts tell us. In 2004 Salman Khan's young cousin, Nadia, came to stay and he helped her with her homework. After she went home he coached her by telephone and later he began to help the children of other friends and relatives. Using the Yahoo! Doodle program, he created simple but effective videos – his voice over a black screen with colour drawings – to keep the lessons going. Nadia found that she preferred this approach to the live tutoring sessions because she could watch them again and again and take things at her own pace. In November 2006, Khan uploaded the first video to a relatively new website called YouTube. It turned out to be the launch of what is now known as the Khan Academy, a free educational site with over 4,000 videos, which has delivered more than 240 million lessons both to adults and children. (I should add that Khan decided to turn it into a not-for-profit business.)

Khan didn't know beforehand that he was launching anything. He was just meeting the needs of his cousin. This highlights another point: you don't have to have any particular business experience or set of skills to launch out on your own; you can slip into business by whatever route you choose. It doesn't matter what your motivation is, either. In my own case, as I have already mentioned, I wanted to help nurse the village where I was born back to life. That meant creating employment, improving the services (such as the shop and bar) and building homes for new residents to live in. There are all sorts of reasons why accidental entrepreneurs launch businesses, but typically it is because we:

- Have been made redundant and can't face hunting for another job
- Have invented a product and want other people to benefit from it
- Want to correct some social wrong
- Have an idea and are interested to see if it will work
- Need to create employment for a relation or friend
- Have a dream we yearn to follow
- Are trying to raise money for a cause

This leads to a slightly different approach to commerce, in which we:

- Only start businesses we really believe in with a passion
- Put financial considerations last
- Put building relationships (especially with customers) first
- Don't pay much attention to what other people think or say
- Trust our instincts
- Do what we feel is right for us
- Are willing to admit our own shortcomings
- Have a great deal of fun

By taking the road less travelled, accidental entrepreneurs bypass many of the problems that other entrepreneurs suffer from, such as worrying about what will happen if the business fails or about losing money. When you have finished this book you'll understand why.

20

The Joy of Business

You can talk about it, read about it and even watch other people doing it, but nothing beats the pleasure of owning your own business. I didn't plan it, but once it happened (you may want to reach for a sick bag at this juncture) I felt an immense sense of freedom. Why did it make me so happy? More than anything else I appreciated having total control over my work life. I enjoyed the variety. As an entrepreneur one wears many hats. And a wholly unexpected benefit turns out to be the intellectual stimulation of being in business.

It is stimulating in another way, too. As an entrepreneur you enjoy the rewards of your own labour. I am not obsessed with money but the truth is, unless you are exceptionally lucky or possess extraordinary talent, owning a business is the best way to build personal wealth.

Risk? What Risk?

There may be some strong and enticing arguments for launching a business, but many would-be entrepreneurs are put off by the perceived risks. I use the word 'perceived' advisedly. Once analysed, many of the dangers associated with being in business, as I am about to explain, are negligible. Let me put your mind to rest regarding any fears you may have.

How to Avoid Financial Risk

'But business is so risky.' If I have heard it once, I have heard it a thousand times. The speaker is under the erroneous impression that entrepreneurs are taking some huge financial risk. In a way I wish this were true as it creates a rather heroic image of us that I am, with regret, about to explode.

Based on hard experience, my strong advice to any new entrepreneur is never to invest more in starting up your business than you can afford to lose. If you can only afford to lose, say, €100, that's fine; I'll show you how to start a business for €100. By adopting this policy you eliminate all the financial risk. Honestly. 'Ah ha,' you might be saying to yourself, 'but what about businesses that need a substantial sum of money to get them off the ground? That will mean risk.' Personally, I would think twice before starting a business that needed more money than I could afford to find myself, but if I was absolutely set on launching something capital-intensive, I would involve one or more external investors. I still wouldn't put in more than I could afford to lose myself. Naturally, you don't want your investors to lose their money and so you need to be absolutely sure they understand the risk involved and – I say this from personal experience – make sure your investors know they are putting up risk equity and not giving you a personal loan.

Of Course You Can Do It

Some would-be entrepreneurs are nervous they won't measure up. Let me assure you: you will. The reason I am so confident is because the business you are going to start will be tailor-made for you. It is going to take full advantage of your exact skills, personality, experience and expertise. For this reason alone you need not worry about being unable to make a go of it. Anyway, if there is something you don't know how to do, simply ask – or employ – someone who does.

Forget Everyone Else

Another concern I have heard voiced by would-be entrepreneurs is that some dreadful event, over which the business has no control, will put the kibosh on everything. There is always, of course, a chance that Earth will be attacked by aliens or hit by a stray meteor, but the more likely possibilities can be planned for. As you build your business you need to regularly assess the risks. List off the various disasters that could occur, decide how likely they really are, and then work out what you would do if each of them actually happened. Imagine you're running a food business. Your three greatest concerns might be: you won't be able to get the ingredients you need; ingredient prices will go through the roof; or you'll have a food safety scare on your hands. These eventualities can all be planned for.

You Can Keep Your Fuel

A man driving through the country late at night suddenly noticed that he was about to run out of fuel. It was a rather wild and remote area and he was pleased to see a light on in a farmhouse. He decided that he would go and ask the owners for some fuel. However, as he drove up the rutted track to the house he began to worry. It was very late. He would probably be waking them up. They would be in a dreadful temper by the time they answered the door. He pictured himself suffering a great deal of verbal abuse and maybe worse. He stayed in his car for a few moments before he summoned up the courage to ring the bell and by the time the door was answered he was in such a state of apprehension that he blurted out, 'You can keep your fuel!'

I bring up this story because it illustrates, perfectly, the dangers of anticipating other people's response. Time and again I have heard people say that they don't want to start a business because if it failed they would be embarrassed. Embarrassment is – like low self-esteem or depression – one of those emotions where there is almost no point in someone telling you that you shouldn't feel it. So, instead, I'll tell you what happened when something I was involved with came to a sticky end. Failing at something is a massive deal for the person involved but of negligible interest to pretty much everyone else. Friends, family, associates, colleagues, the media – in fact, the entire world – pay almost no attention whatsoever to the event. One's immediate family may notice but, honestly, even they tend to say very little. Moreover, the few people who do make reference to it are always sympathetic. I mean *always*. The world loves a trier. I have never once felt any sense of embarrassment when one of my ventures has had to be put quietly to sleep. In fact, my emotions tend to be relief and expectation, because when one door closes another opens. If you fail (and, as I explain in Chapter 28, there is much to be said for failure) you may also be surprised at how quickly you get over it.

Another Sort of Risk

There is something else I would like you to consider. Has it occurred to you that there could be a risk in *not* starting a business? Put bluntly, we all have a limited lifespan. There are things we can do to extend it, such as living well, eating healthily and taking exercise, but basically it is what it is. In fact, the only thing we can really do is ensure that we use our time on earth wisely. Put another way, one of the greatest risks we all have as human beings is wasting time doing something that we don't feel strongly about, let alone love. When you are old it would be a shame to be sitting in your chair wishing that you had been bolder. The American author Chuck Palahniuk said something appropriate in this regard:

> If you knew that your life was merely a phase or short, short segment of your entire existence, how would you live? Knowing nothing 'real' was at risk, what would you do? You'd live a gigantic, bold, fun, dazzling life. You know you would. That's what the ghosts want us to do – all the exciting things they no longer can.

Whether you work for a private enterprise or the government, the days of job security are now long gone. Indeed, if security is what you are after, what could be more secure than owning your own successful business? Without wishing to come over all spiritual, by remaining an employee you may be doing terrible things to your soul. As another writer, Anaïs Nin, says, 'And the day came when the risk to remain tight in the bud was more painful than the risk it took to blossom.'

21

WHAT'S THE BIG IDEA?

I firmly believe that if you find something you love, the money will follow. Clearly, however, some business ideas are better than others. The objective, therefore, is to launch a business you love and that is also based on a really good idea. Of course, ideas are simply ideas and, as such, have only moderate value. It is all in the execution. If I told you that you could make a fortune launching a business that produced jam, you probably wouldn't be that impressed. After all, it doesn't sound like much of a plan. However, that's exactly what a fourteen-year-old schoolboy called Fraser Doherty did after being taught to make jam by his grandmother.

Scottish-born Doherty called his company SuperJam and from day one he focused on producing a range of 100 per cent pure fruit jams, sweetened with grape juice and made using 'super fruits', such as blueberries and cranberries. He started out selling his produce at farmers' markets and to local delicatessens. It took him two years to set up a proper production facility, create a brand and perfect his recipes, at which point he became the youngest ever supplier to the UK supermarket chain Waitrose. SuperJam now sells through more than 2,000 supermarkets around the world and turns over millions of pounds a year. Moreover, the company has shaken up the entire jam market through its use of quality ingredients and innovative recipes. SuperJam makes substantial donations to charity, sponsors regular tea dances for the elderly and has developed an interesting sideline in merchandising.

I can't think of a better illustration of my point: it wasn't Doherty's *idea* that was particularly unique, it was the *way he executed it*.

Ideas Are the Beginning, Not the End

Coming up with a winning idea is, then, simply a beginning, not an end. If you are going to make your idea work you need to spend time giving it thought, doing research, working out a strategy and producing a simple business plan. From personal experience I would warn against flitting from idea to idea. To move forward it is important to focus on one concept at a time and to examine it thoroughly from every angle. Actually, I would go further than this. The best way to decide if your idea is any good is to put it to the test.

Putting Your Idea to the Test

There is no idea – no matter how complicated or capital-intensive – that cannot be tested before you invest in it. You might think it is much easier to test, say, a raspberry and cranberry jam recipe than an unbuilt hotel, but it isn't. You just need a different approach. In the case of the jam you could make up sample batches to sell or give away. From the response you get you will easily be able to tell whether the recipe is likely to prove popular. In the case of the unbuilt hotel the boldest option would be to pretend it already existed and to run some small advertisements in appropriate magazines to see if you receive any bookings. An alternative would be to produce a presentation with a view to generating advance sales from within the travel trade. You could also show the presentation to prospective guests to gauge their response. Whether you are selling a product or a service (or both), by testing it first you will either get the confidence you require to continue or – just as usefully – you will know that you need to rethink your plans. Either way, this is perhaps the most vital stage of developing a new business.

Consider Scalability

The best business ideas are scalable. In other words, if the concept is a success it will be easy to make the business grow. Some businesses are easier to scale than others. Let's say that your passion is model railway sets. You decide that you are going to start creating tiny figures of passengers to sell to fellow enthusiasts. There are probably more model railway enthusiasts than one imagines but this is still a niche market. Bluntly, even if sales are good there is nowhere for you to go. On the other hand, suppose you create cute miniature dolls that can be dressed up, together with a wide range of ever-changing accessories. If your market, girls aged between three and ten, falls in love with your toys, there is huge potential for expansion. Generally speaking it's the size of your market that determines the scalability of your business.

The Importance of Solving a Problem

Take up one idea. Make that one idea your life – think of it, dream of it, live on that idea. Let the brain, muscles, nerves, every part of your body, be full of that idea, and just leave every other idea alone. This is the way to success.

That quote does not come from a business leader but from an Indian Hindu monk called Swami Vivekananda. I don't completely agree with the swami, because I think it is actually important to enrich one's own life and the lives of others in many different ways, but I do like the way he exhorted his supporters to throw themselves into whatever they were doing. The problem is, of course, choosing something worth throwing yourself into. Specifically, when choosing a business to start, how can you be certain that it is a winner?

In a strange way, all businesses solve problems. You might ask yourself what problem a company like SuperJam is solving – after all, consumers didn't appear to be crying out for another brand of jam – but, actually, it appears they were. None of the big manufacturers were making 100 per cent fruit jam and this created a real opening in the market – which goes to show that just because the opportunity isn't obvious doesn't mean it isn't there. By and large, entrepreneurs focus on their solutions rather than on the problems they are trying to alleviate. This is understandable. If you come up with a wizard product or service, naturally you want to refine it. Nevertheless, I would urge you not to lose sight of your customers' needs. Let me give you an example.

Home Depot, an American company, runs the largest chain of DIY stores in the world. On the face of it you might think that they are in the business of retailing products. After all, homeowners come to them to buy a wide range of items, from baths to barbecues and from wheelbarrows to windows. In fact, you would only be half right. What Home Depot's customers really want is to solve some sort of household problem. Their wiring needs replacing or their roof leaks or they want a new patio. Home Depot recognised this and now it provides a range of building services. In fact, this is the fastest growing area of its business and its CEO believes that it will become the most profitable thing the company has ever done.

The Importance of a Unique Selling Proposition

In the 1960s an advertising executive called Rosser Reeves came up with a concept called the unique selling proposition, or USP. Customers need, he said, to understand what benefit you are offering them and also what makes you different from your competition. When evaluating your own idea, therefore, it is worth spending some time considering what USP your product or service offers.

One of the most obvious benefits is innovation. The American writer and poet Ralph Waldo Emerson summed it up when he supposedly said, 'Build a better mousetrap, and the world will beat a path to your door.' (His actual quote is not so pithy, but you get the point.) If you have an innovative product then, really, there is no more to be said. You are set.

Another possible benefit is price; the idea that if you build a *cheaper* mousetrap the world will beat a path to your door. There is some truth in this, but I always feel that it is a shaky foundation on which to build a business empire. I must admit this is partly because I have an aversion to lower-quality products, a natural result of trying to maintain low prices. There is also the risk, when you sell on price, that someone will undercut you. Anyway, in my experience, people who buy on price are rarely very loyal.

What about scarcity value? This can take many forms, but one example is the shops in airports, which are able to command much higher prices because there is no effective competition. There are many successful businesses built on scarcity value, but I do feel they are vulnerable to unexpected competition.

You could consider making service your USP, and I would strongly endorse such a move. If you look after your customers, build a relationship with them and listen to what they say, you will engender a high level of loyalty and thus be able to rely on their continued support. There isn't a customer in the world who doesn't appreciate it if you go out of your way to make sure that they are satisfied with the products or service you are offering. Not only will happy customers keep coming back, but they will also recommend you. Build your business on the back of first-class service and I am willing to guarantee its prosperity and longevity.

As an aside, there is another advantage to offering good service. If you operate in a market where there is almost no difference between your product and your competitors' it gives you an edge. At one point, Guinness, the brewery, stopped all its advertising and invested in customer research and training. Up until that point sales had been declining steadily. After that year, armed with a much better understanding of their market and having trained thousands and thousands of barmen and women all over the world on how to serve their product, Guinness sales exploded.

There is one final USP that you can use to great advantage if you want to build a successful business: quality. Although producing a higher-quality product or service means higher costs, it also means much happier customers.

Consider Going into the Fish Business

When it comes to assessing your business idea, there is one other tip I want to offer you. You have probably heard the expression, 'If you give a man a fish, you feed him for a day; if you teach him to fish, you feed him for life.' In my experience, in the developed Western world, a high percentage of consumers would rather be given a cooked fish than be taught how to fish. A fantastic example of this can be seen in the retail food business. Most supermarkets now offer a wide range of prepared food including such items as mashed potato, tomato sauce, cucumber relish and chicken stock. As all these items can be produced at home quickly and extremely inexpensively, it never fails to amaze me that people are willing to pay such a high premium to have it done for them. They are, however, and perhaps it is only right to satisfy them.

What to Do if You're Stuck

Suppose you haven't hit on an idea that really excites you. Begin by thinking hard about what you are good at, what you could become good at and what you love. This may help you decide what sort of general area you want your business to operate in. Day-to-day life is, for me, a rich source of new business ideas. Every time I read a newspaper, go shopping, search online, chat with friends, boil a kettle, clean my teeth, drive somewhere, watch television, listen to the radio … every single waking moment, in fact, I am looking around me to see where there might be a potential opportunity. I also read trade publications, visit trade exhibitions and canvas the opinion of almost everyone I meet. You would be amazed what people will tell you if you ask nicely. I constantly monitor my own reactions. What is worrying me? What do I like? What annoys me? How could something I am doing be improved? Incidentally, if you are looking for ideas, pay special attention to businesses in other countries. If it works there, maybe it would work where you live.

A Few More Hints

J. Paul Getty, the Texan oil billionaire, said, 'Formula for success: rise early, work hard, strike oil.' Easy for him to say. What about the rest of us? Here are some tips.

Never Be Afraid to Steal the Latest

This was something that Leo Burnett, founder of the eponymous advertising agency (once the largest in the world) used to tell his creative staff. It is a myth that all entrepreneurs are good at generating brilliant ideas. The best entrepreneurs are simply brilliant at making things happen. So don't be ashamed of looking to other people and their businesses for inspiration. Richard Branson didn't come up with the idea of launching an airline; rather, someone who owned a plane came to him and asked if he had any ideas about what could be done with it.

Ask Lots of Questions

When I was planning GreatGas, one of the biggest challenges I faced was finding a company willing to supply me with fuel. I had no idea how the market worked or who I should approach. I know it sounds so basic but I found the information I needed just by asking questions of people who might know.

Stick to What You Know

I don't want to sound too unkind, but the fact is that the chance of you coming up with a new idea that people love and no one has thought of in an industry you know nothing about is – bluntly – almost non-existent. Stick to what you know. For instance, I know about branding and marketing, so while I might go into businesses as varied as oil and clinical medicine, I go in wearing my branding and marketing hat. Also, if you want to get into something new, spend your time really learning about it first. The road to insolvency is paved with stories of amateurs who thought they could go professional in an area they really knew nothing about.

Beware of Fads

Do you remember pet rocks? The chap who came up with the concept made a million … and then the business folded. Why? Because pet rocks were a fad. Any fad business is always going to be short term and potentially risky. Also, bear in mind that the world is constantly evolving and if you want to stay in business you need to be conscious of change and change with it.

Look for Periods of Change

We are in a period of change at the moment and as a result, in my opinion, there are some amazing opportunities. What sort of period of change are we in? Primarily, economic and technological. But there are always other, less obvious sorts of change taking place, for instance when new legislation comes in or when customers alter their buying habits. The advice 'look for a gap in the market' is sound. But, perhaps it would be better rephrased as 'look for a *large* gap in the market.' If there isn't sufficient business to be won, the gap is as good as worthless.

Can You Put a Spin on an Existing Business?

You don't always have to reinvent the wheel; sometimes taking an existing business and putting a novel spin on it can ensure success. It may be an urban myth, but it is said that NASA invested millions of dollars in designing a pen that would work properly in space where there is no gravity to push the ink down the tube. The Russians, on the other hand, used a pencil! As Albert Einstein pointed out, 'There is nothing that is a more certain sign of insanity than to do the same thing over and over and expect the results to be different.' I mention this because you are unlikely to come up with a new, creative idea if you get locked into a cycle of thinking.

Make or Buy?

This is the single biggest question that every entrepreneur faces. In other words, is it better to start a new business from scratch or to buy an existing business in the sector you want to get into and expand it? Many people believe that it is cheaper to make than to buy, but in my experience this isn't always the case. Companies that are for sale may, for one reason or another, be seriously undervalued. Furthermore, it is sometimes possible to purchase a business on much better terms than one might previously have imagined. In particular, where the vendor is under pressure to sell it is often possible to do a deal that allows you to pay for the business over time. A good tactic might be to take an option on the shares in a company so that you have the ability to buy it at a later date at an agreed price if you so choose. This sort of deal can be very useful because it allows you to really understand the nuts and bolts of a business and to see what you can do with it before you have to put most of your money down. Of course, the vendor has to trust you not to make any mistakes with the business while you are running it and so it takes a responsible, honest and credible purchaser to make this sort of deal work out.

Call Yourself in for an Interview

If I was asked to recommend the single most valuable thing any would-be entrepreneur could do to improve his or her chances of success it would be this: interview yourself for the job. The primary purpose of the interview is to establish whether you have the right personality, skills and resources to start your proposed business. Here are some of the questions you might ask yourself.

- What are you good at?
- What do you love doing?
- What special skills do you have?
- Do you have any relevant experience?
- How much time can you put into this business?
- How much money can you put into this business?
- Do you have access to any other non-financial resources (such as property or equipment) that would be useful to the business?
- Do you have any useful contacts that would help the business?
- What sort of personality would you say you have?
- Do you think you have the right personality for this job?
- Do you feel passionate about this particular business idea (and, if so, why)?
- Can you see yourself running this business in three years' time? In five years? Ten years?

Creating a business is a wonderful opportunity to create a work environment that really suits you. You don't have to have all the required resources and skills yourself – it is enough that you are the sort of person who will be able to go out and find them.

22

WHY A RECESSION IS THE ACCIDENTAL ENTREPRENEUR'S FRIEND

'If I could start again, I would set up all my businesses during recessions,' Richard Branson told readers of the *Telegraph* in 2012, 'as such a climate is perfect for young, enthusiastic and nimble companies to thrive.' In fact, I don't think there is ever a bad time to start a good business. But there are definitely some distinct advantages to launching a new venture when the economy is in poor shape.

All the evidence indicates that companies founded during downturns have greater longevity and produce higher profits. Indeed, when the Kauffman Foundation sponsored a 2009 study into the early origins of America's largest corporations, as listed on the Fortune 500 list, it transpired that more than half were launched during a recession or bear market. When you consider that the US economy was only in recession for around thirteen years in the period from 1900 to 2009, it is clear that a troubled economy is the accidental entrepreneur's best friend.

Why should this be? Broadly speaking I believe it is because such companies tend to be a much more mindful of how they spend their money. When times are good start-ups often flash their cash, but when times are hard they make do on a shoestring budget. Leaner companies are more resilient too. The management is used to coping with tough markets and a shortage of cash and as a result it is more creative and dogged. Let's face it, if you manage to start a business and survive a severe downturn, the chances are that you are really going to flourish when times are good.

There are multiple businesses that have thrived in a recession, like, for instance, Women's Fitness Plus. Noel Smyth and Michael Melleney purchased this business in Cork city at the height of the Irish recession in 2010. Smyth and Melleney bought the business as an investment and envisaged that it would give them both an extra income. The business struggled initially but once Smyth decided to work full-time in the business he and Melleney discovered that even with an economic downturn women's fitness was an industry that had plenty of room for growth in Ireland. Concentrating on what they had learned from the previous businesses they had worked in, they managed to grow almost immediately. In fact, they had doubled in size after two years and bought another gym in Limerick in 2013.

Another Irish business that proves you can open and prosper in a recession is Great National Hotels and Resorts. In 2010 it became apparent to hotelier David Byrne and his colleague David Collins that international hotel brands and loose hotel marketing associations were either too expensive, with overly demanding terms and conditions, or not effective in the fight for diminishing market share. These two issues – coupled with the needs of large independent hotels to avail of group management structures, group purchasing, group marketing and, critically, help in tackling the growth of online sales channels – gave birth to the idea for Great National Hotels and Resorts. From just one part-time employee in 2010, Great National now employs 35 expert personnel at their central head office in Ennis and has multiple hotels under management.

How to Make Your Business Recession-Proof

If you are in the unfortunate position of owning a business that has been hit by a downturn, the last thing you want to be told is how you could have made it recession-proof before the economy tanked. But if you haven't yet launched your business you are in a very different position. Put the following measures in place to ensure that the business you are building is strong enough to weather any future storms.

Plan for the Worst, Hope for the Best

The more experienced I get in business, the more important I believe it is to have a financial safety net in place so that if, for example, sales or profits are lower than anticipated (or if costs are higher) it won't catch you off-guard. Even if you don't have a cash reserve of your own you can still create a safety net. One option is to get pre-approval for a loan or overdraft that, with luck, you will never have to call upon. Another option is to line up investors willing to give you cash should you ever need it. Keep yourself lean, too. Do you really need that extra employee? Could you make do with less expensive premises? Would second-hand equipment do the job just as well? It is prudent planning to run a tight ship. Incidentally, if your colleagues and employees know that you don't waste money, they won't waste money either.

Avoid Unprofitable Customers

It is always tempting to take all the business you are offered. But, the reality is that a percentage of your customers will always be unprofitable. Therefore, it is important to make sure that every single sale you make is contributing to your bottom line. Moreover, be careful about who you extend credit to. There is no point in making a sale if you never get paid.

Mind Your Customers

There are hundreds and hundreds of books about customer care and customer management. Don't spend too much of your time reading them. You wouldn't, after all, read a book about how to be a good friend, would you? And being a good friend is really all you need to do to establish long-lasting and mutually advantageous relationships with your customers. In fact, if you don't think of them as customers but as people you like and respect – people you are happy to go out of your way to help – you'll be well on the way to recession-proofing your business. I like to surprise customers if I can. Once I got an email from someone who wanted to buy a copy of *The Annals of Churchtown*. As it happened I was about to drive close to where he lived and had a copy in my car, so half an hour after he contacted me I was ringing his doorbell to deliver it.

Invest

Koch Industries, one of the largest privately held corporations in the world, with annual revenue, more or less, of $100 billion, increases, not decreases, its investment during every recession. It is part of its strategy to increase spending when others are cutting costs. In particular, it invests in advertising and marketing because it knows that during a downturn many large businesses pull back on their communication budgets, which in turn opens up new opportunities. The proof of the pudding is in the eating: Koch has grown seven times faster than the S&P 500 over the past four decades.

Employ the Best

Don't be a prima donna. One of the worst mistakes any entrepreneur can make is to believe that no one can do a job as well as they can. If you want your business to grow and prosper I strongly recommend delegating to your employees and letting them learn from their mistakes. They may not be as good as you, but they will get better. Of course, ideally you should be employing people who are better than yourself. Also, it is better to get rid of anyone who doesn't measure up. An executive at Apple Inc. is credited with saying, 'Better to have a hole than an asshole.' I agree with him. Someone who isn't working with you is, effectively, working against you.

Look for Strategic Partnerships

There is an Asian saying, 'Before you can multiply, you must first learn to divide.' In other words, if you want to build anything you must accept a smaller share. I do and don't agree with this. There are times when it is advantageous to have partners and times when one is better off on one's own. However, there are many different types of partner and not all of them require a reduction in your own equity. For example, you could team up with a non-competitive business selling into the same market as yourself. By working together you could reduce your costs and improve your efficiency.

Work Your Cash Harder

More than once I have been involved with a profitable business that was unable to expand because it didn't have sufficient cash to fund its operations. It is only too easy, as an entrepreneur, to look at the profit margin and forget that you may have to meet the cost of a sale long before you receive any income from it. With this in mind, watch your cash flow like a hawk. If your customers pay you a long time after you have had to pay your creditors, make sure your prices are high enough to allow for the cost of credit.

Watch Your Figures

Over the years I have gradually learned that one can save a lot of time by working out what the key performance indicators (KPIs) are for any given business. For instance, in one of my companies I look at sales closed but not yet fulfilled as a way of estimating which way that particular company is going to go. Leonard Lauder, the chairman of Estée Lauder, noticed that after the terrorist attacks of 11 September 2001 his company was selling more lipstick than usual. He theorised that lipstick purchases were a way to gauge not just the health of his company but also the health of the economy. When things are shaky, he said, sales increase 'as women boost their mood with inexpensive lipstick purchases instead of $500 shoes'.

Recession-Proof Businesses

Finding a sector that won't be affected by a recession is the Holy Grail for many entrepreneurs. As it happens, there are some types of business that definitely seem to hold up better – and even to flourish – during economic turmoil. Although, having said this, my own view is that if you have built a strong, healthy, resilient organisation you have no need to worry about the economy. After all, most developed nations experience recessions for only 5 to 10 per cent of the time. To choose a business concept specifically because it may do well during these periods strikes me as silly.

Still, if you want to plan for the worst, consider a business that provides critical repair and maintenance services; serves a customer base that is unaffected by recession; provides products or services that are paid for by government regulation or compliance rules; or that are market leaders in their field, offering such high-quality goods and services that customers are always reluctant to leave.

23

How to Start a Business on a Shoestring

Starbucks, the international chain of coffee shops, was launched by three academics, each of whom invested $1,350 of their own money to open the first outlet in downtown Seattle. Mattel, best known for its Barbie dolls, was started in the founders' garage. Apple, the computer company with an estimated value of $580 billion, also started life in a garage. Houston-born John Mackey, the co-founder of the Whole Foods supermarket chain, had so little money to start his first shop that he slept in the stockroom for the first year in order to save on rent.

It is a complete and total fallacy that you need lots of capital to start a business. Many of the most successful companies in the world had very modest beginnings. Even ventures that would appear to require a vast amount of funding, such as hospitals or oil companies, can be launched on a shoestring if you are suitably creative.

You might think that the primary benefit of starting a business on a shoestring is that it will save you money. What it actually does, however, is force you to build a better model with a sustainable cash flow. With no money to waste, you will waste no money. This in turn will substantially reduce your stress levels. After all, if you haven't got a lot of money riding on the success of your business you have much less to worry about. Why start a business that requires a huge investment when you can start one that doesn't? Also, why seek outside investors if you can keep all the shares and fund it yourself? Here are 21 tips to help you get launched for next to nothing.

1. *Don't prevaricate:* As soon as you possibly can, start selling your product or service. Why? Because it will bring in valuable income. Too many entrepreneurs wait until everything is perfect before they launch. When Steve Wozniak and Steve Jobs founded Apple they built a prototype and took it to a local storeowner, who immediately ordered fifty. Jobs and Wozniak then persuaded a local computer parts supplier to give them everything they needed on credit and they started building the computers in Wozniak's garage. There is a great deal to be said for selling first and working out how you are going to fulfil the orders afterwards.

2. *Discover what your prospective customers think before you launch:* If you are planning to manufacture a product, produce a prototype. If you are planning something substantial like a hotel or hospital, get a student or artist to create a video or drawings to explain it. Whatever you are planning, work out some way to show it to your prospective customers first and get feedback. They will either give you the confidence to proceed or, if the response is poor, stop you wasting your money.

3. *Keep the day job:* If you are currently in paid employment, don't give up your job to launch your business; start it in your spare time.

4. *Be innovative:* Make creativity your currency. It would normally take tens of millions of euros to launch an oil distribution company. I started mine with €3,749. I couldn't afford to buy storage facilities, delivery trucks or petrol stations. Instead I formed a buying group of independent petrol stations and negotiated with other companies to supply us, taking a small percentage off the top.

5. *Remember, you are your own best employee:* Don't pay someone else to do a job that you could possibly do yourself for free. Don't be proud. If you can save by cleaning or painting the office or business premises at the weekend, just do it. You won't look foolish; people will actually admire you.

6. *Rope in friends and family:* Ask your friends and family to help you get launched.

7. *Launch from home:* Is there any way you could start your business from your home? Not only will it save you having to pay rent, but because it eliminates commuting it will mean you can spend more time developing your concept.

8. *Beg, borrow and barter:* I recently read about a woman who was launching a bakery. As she couldn't afford commercial premises and equipment she did a deal with a local restaurant whereby she used their kitchen from midnight until seven in the morning. She paid her rent in the form of free bread and pastries. If you need something – whether it is equipment, premises, ingredients or materials – consider whether there is someone who might lend or give it to you.

9. *Work smarter:* You will get much more done if you prioritise your tasks and manage your time well. There may be lots of things you feel you ought to do that can, in fact, be postponed. The less time you waste on unnecessary activities, and the more efficient you are, the sooner your start-up will be up and running and the less investment you will need.

10. *Learn to shop:* I once had to buy some office furniture. If I had bought the pieces I really wanted it would have cost me more than €20,000. Even going to a chain store the bill would have been €4,000. In the end I bought everything I needed second-hand for a little over €2,000. Whether you need a paper clip or a container ship there is always a way to buy it more cheaply. Incidentally, beating the supplier's price down so they make little or no profit is generally self-defeating. Remember, one day you may need the supplier to help you out of a jam with repairs or a rush order. Being aggressive towards suppliers is not the way of the accidental entrepreneur.

11. *Find yourself a mentor:* You can learn from books, of course, but nothing beats one-to-one support from an experienced teacher. Find one or more entrepreneurs with relevant expertise to guide you through the start-up process. Most mentors are happy to be asked and will do what they can free of charge. Incidentally, if you

pick the right mentors they may also bring in new customers for you.

12. *See if what you need is available free:* Perhaps it is not surprising given the amount of wealth in the developed world, but there are vast resources sitting around unused. Recently, the 'freecycle' movement has tried to capitalise on this by encouraging people with redundant assets to give them away. The Freecycle Network is made up of 5,146 groups with 7,746,553 members around the world. It is a grassroots and entirely non-profit movement of people who are giving (and getting) stuff for free in their own towns. It's all about reusing and keeping good stuff out of landfills. You would be surprised what you can get for free.

13. *Get your customers to fund your working capital:* Property developers do this when they sell off-plan. Tailors ask you to do it when they look for a deposit before they start work. And if you visit the Kickstarter website you will see that hundreds of artisan manufacturers are pre-selling their products before they have even made them. If you are looking to keep your costs down, why not see if you can get your future customers to provide you with some of the money you require?

14. *Sell or give away equity:* If you can't afford to employ the person you want and/or buy the equipment you need, consider bartering shares in your new business. Take professional advice first, however, as you don't want to find yourself saddled with nuisance shareholders.

15. *Budget:* Really work out your figures. How little can you get the business launched for? Pay particular attention to cash flow. If you are starting your business over several months you may not need all the money at once.

16. *Work backwards:* I often do my budget backwards. I begin with the amount of money I have to launch my business and then allocate it to the various things I need to pay for. I find this exercise often makes me more creative.

17. *Get your suppliers to fund your business:* As I have already mentioned, supplier funding – possibly in the form of credit, possibly in the form of goods or services – is generally an inexpensive

way to fund a start-up. A typical example is where a retailer is given goods on sale or return, or where an equipment supplier takes payment over time.

18. *Don't forget free money:* Depending on where you live there may be all sorts of government grants, tax incentives and schemes designed to help you keep costs down. Personally, I avoid such funding because the bureaucracy involved makes the process slow and frustrating. However, there are situations where it makes sound sense.

19. *Make do:* I have already mentioned the importance of shopping around and spending as little as possible. I have also suggested that you get what you can for free. Another tactic I suggest is simply making do with something that is less than perfect.

20. *Use profits to fund growth:* Use the profits your business generates to fund its ongoing expansion.

21. *Fail quickly:* Most businesses take several years to become profitable. However, if a business idea is clearly not working, close it down quickly before you lose more than you need to. If a business is doomed it is better to accept it sooner rather than later.

24

THE ETHICAL ADVANTAGE

Ever since the Body Shop was founded in the 1970s, an increasing number of entrepreneurs have chosen to launch socially responsible businesses. Such businesses outperform purely profit-driven ventures (I'll come back to this in a moment), proving that it is possible both to make money and make a difference. Before I explain all the benefits of incorporating a strong ethical element into your own business, let me offer you a few examples:

- When you buy a pair of shoes from TOMS they give a pair away to someone in need and when you buy a pair of their sunglasses they help to save or restore someone's sight. The company also campaigns for fair wages for workers and against human trafficking and slavery.
- Madécasse is a chocolate company founded by two US Peace Corps volunteers that makes and packages its entire range in Madagascar. It goes 'beyond fair trade' in terms of paying workers and creating employment and it also conserves the environment and improves biodiversity.
- Divine, another chocolate producer, has actually given shares to the farmers who produce the cocoa.
- Satya Jewelry ('satya' means 'truth' in Sanskrit) was started by two friends who wanted to support children's charities in developing nations. So far they have donated over $1 million to good causes.

- Ecoigo is a London-based limousine service that only uses environmentally friendly vehicles, offsets 100 per cent of its carbon and makes sizeable charitable donations every year.
- The John Lewis Partnership, the third-largest privately held company in the UK, consists of a chain of eponymous department stores and a chain of food stores (Waitrose). The son of the original founder effectively gave the business to the staff in 1929 (although he carried on running and expanding it until 1955) and since 1950 it has been an employee-managed partnership. The chain, which is well known for its ethical sourcing and pricing policies, is a wonderful example of how turning employees into owners can produce a highly profitable and yet socially responsible business.

These examples all incorporate ethics into their ordinary commercial activities. Some socially responsible businesses, however, were started purely in order to pursue a social, moral and/or environmental programme. My favourite example of this is Dr Bronner's Magic Soap. The Dr Bronner after whom the soap is named was a third-generation Jewish master soap maker from a tiny little town in Germany. In the late 1920s he emigrated to America, where he began lecturing about 'The Moral ABC', his plan for achieving world peace. As a thank you to the people who came to listen to him he used to hand out a free bar of soap. After a while he realised that people were coming for the soap, not the lectures, so he printed the lecture on the packaging and started selling the soap. Today Dr Bronner's turns over $50 million a year and is managed by the founder's grandson. Pretty much all the profits are given away to charity and the business is run for the benefit of the employees, not the shareholders. For instance, the highest-paid executive can't earn more than five times the lowest-paid employee. Interestingly, the company never spends a single penny on advertising or marketing.

Why Being Good Pays

I became an entrepreneur myself by accident, while working on a rural renewal project. This isn't quite the same as a socially responsible business, of course, but it stems from the same philosophy of combining ethical and profit motives. This is why I am so keen to persuade you to run a socially responsible business:

- It is immensely rewarding. It is infinitely more satisfying to promote a service or product that benefits other people or the planet.
- Consumer interest in this area is huge. Businesses that are not-just-for-profit tap into a huge community of customers who choose where to spend their money based primarily on their principles.
- You will experience greater customer loyalty. When a business and its customers share the same principles and values there is a much stronger relationship. Like attracts like.
- Your customers will promote your business for you. Ethical businesses frequently don't have to spend a penny on advertising or marketing because all their customers come by word of mouth.
- Employees will love you. People prefer to work for a company that is helping others or the planet and they may even be willing to work for less because of it.
- The media will love you. You can look forward to much higher levels of media coverage. Getting publicity for your business will be considerably easier.
- It will help you differentiate your product or service from those of your competition. Given a choice of two identical products, one ethically produced and one not, consumers will opt for the one with the socially responsible story.
- It is much easier to raise money. Oddly enough, investors and banks really love ethical businesses – perhaps because they know they tend to be better run and more profitable.

Why Ethical Companies Make More Money

A good way to understand why ethical companies do better than their less ethical counterparts is to study the ethical investment sector. Its history can be traced back to the nineteenth century when religious groups, most noticeably the Quakers and Methodists, recommended that their adherents withhold investment from companies that didn't embrace temperance and fair employment conditions. In the 1980s the anti-apartheid movement and environmental concerns gave ethical investment a huge boost and a large number of specialist funds were established. Today around one-sixth of all US managed funds are invested in companies with a high degree of social responsibility. If you look at the overall statistics, ethical funds have produced above average returns, even allowing for the costs of extra screening. Many funds perform even better. It appears that companies with strong ethical principles tend to be better run and less hampered by regulatory, legal and publicity problems.

What Does 'Socially Responsible' Mean?

There are lots of different terms in use to describe not-just-for-profit businesses, including 'socially responsible businesses', 'ethical businesses' and 'conscious businesses'. Whatever label you apply, to my mind what we are talking about is any commercial organisation that aims to:

- Do no harm to humans or the environment
- Promote a social and/or environmental agenda
- Support one or more social and/or environmental causes
- Achieve a profit

It isn't for everyone. After all, you have to be both an entrepreneur capable of launching a successful business and someone with the skills required to run a not-for-profit. On the other hand, if you get it right your success will be twice as rewarding. Not only should you make money, you will do so in a way that affirms your own core values.

What It Takes

What does it take to launch a socially responsible business? Here are some tips to get you started:

- Just being socially responsible won't bring the customers in. You must still solve their problems and meet their needs. Don't forget business basics. Don't even think about starting a social enterprise without a business plan. No amount of passion for your cause will make up for lack of planning.

- Consider what social or environmental issues are important to you. It could be something like rural renewal, farm animal welfare, the plight of underprivileged women in developing nations or the harmful chemicals used in skincare products. Clearly, it should tie in with your business.
- Set out your ethical values in a document that you can give to customers, the media, investors and so forth. Consider writing an ethical code.
- Decide how far you are willing to go. The range of options is enormous, from making sure that your business is carbon neutral to giving your workers a share in the company and from donating a percentage of your turnover to a charity to campaigning on a political issue.
- Do your research. It is important to choose issues that other people consider important. Remember that if other people don't feel strongly about the same thing, your business is unlikely to be a success.
- Expect to be 100 per cent transparent in whatever it is you are doing. Ethical consumers really study the businesses they give their custom to and if they have cause to believe that you are insincere, dishonest or failing to meet the standards you have set for yourself they will stop buying from you.
- Make sure that your staff not only understand what your business stands for, but that they sign up to it.
- Appoint an independent person or board to oversee what you are doing. It will add to your credibility if you can prove that you are delivering on your promises.

Looking for Ideas

In starting a socially responsible business you are also starting an issue-based business. Being interested in a particular issue might quickly lead to a business idea. For example, Marty Metro, the founder of UsedCardboardBoxes.com, was deeply concerned about the way in which second-hand cardboard boxes were being disposed of by large-scale retailers. Some boxes were ending up in landfill; others were being recycled, but not in an environmentally friendly way. When he came up with an efficient way of collecting, inspecting and re-selling second-hand boxes it was as a direct result of his concern for the environment.

Interestingly, lots of big (but not especially ethical) multinationals are now looking to the developing world for ideas. For example, in Bangladesh a microfinance pioneer called Grameen Bank was funding tiny dairies capable of producing yoghurt to an extremely high standard. The yoghurt was then packed into cooler bags and sold via shops or direct to the public. It was done this way because in Bangladesh there is almost no refrigerated storage. The concept came to the attention of Groupe Danone, which started a joint venture in Bangladesh called EcoPack. They are now considering launching other micro yoghurt and dairy plants in other countries around the world.

Are There Any Catches?

When I launched GreatGas in 2005, we hoped to persuade drivers to modify their vehicles so that they could be powered by plant oil. We converted our company van, struck a deal with a local supplier, put tanks into four of our forecourts and planned to build a plant oil refinery. My efforts resulted in a great deal of publicity but although plant-based fuel offers substantial financial and environmental benefits, consumers were unenthusiastic and in the end – with great regret and a cash loss – I shelved the scheme. This hasn't put me off socially responsible business – far from it – but does underline the fact that being principled does not, in and of itself, guarantee you success.

One point to remember is that when it comes to ethical and environmental issues there isn't always a straightforward answer. Take wood from a sustainable plantation. You might think that this would automatically make it environmentally friendly. However, as part of the production process the timber may have been pressure treated with toxic agents and preservatives. Not so green now, eh? Composite woods may actually be better for the environment. Another thing to be aware of is that consumers are easily confused. It's important to communicate in a way that they can relate to. For example, a study by SC Johnson found that consumers are more likely to act on product benefits such as 'safe to use around children' and 'no toxic ingredients' than benefits such as 'recyclable packaging'.

It Doesn't Have to Be Complicated

Many ethical businesses are extremely simple. Green Depot, for instance, is a building supplies company that only sells environmentally friendly building products. Looptworks upcycles rubbish into fashion items. The IOU Project supports hand-weaving in India. The ecoATM is a machine that pays people to recycle their old electronics. The world is your (ethically farmed) oyster.

25

Honey, I Shrunk the Business Plan

'To achieve great things,' said the American composer Leonard Bernstein, 'two things are needed: a plan and not quite enough time.' I couldn't agree with him more, and because none of us can ever have quite enough time, I urge you not to get too hung up about your business plan. Yes, you need one, but its primary value (unless you are using it to raise money) lies in its preparation, not in the finished document. As you write it you will be forced to think through every aspect of your venture and this – bluntly – will reduce your chances of making a mess of things. Later on, once you get started, my guess is that you will barely refer to it, except possibly as an aide-mémoire. This is because once you finish your business plan you can be absolutely certain that what you have described is the one scenario that will never occur. Helman Von Moltke said it first and Colin Powell repeated it when he said, 'No battle plan survives contact with the enemy.' Incidentally, there is another reason to keep your business plan relatively short. They take time to write: time that may be better spent getting your venture up and running.

The best sort of business plan is concise (clear and waffle-free), not over-emotional (but you do need to demonstrate your passion), logical (to give you and any readers confidence), factual (to prove that you understand the opportunity) and realistic (to show that you have your feet firmly on the ground).

Its purpose is to:

- Prove that the opportunity exists and explain how you plan to exploit it
- Identify any potential problems before you get started
- Show that the business is going to make money – and when
- Help you work out what resources (cash and other) you need until you start making a profit
- Focus your time, energy and money in the most valuable way
- Provide a yardstick against which you can measure success or failure

Obviously if you are self-funding your business the plan need not look that professional. It could be as little as a page or two of notes and figures. If you are using it to raise money it should obviously be somewhat more professional. Actually, a well-presented business plan will be useful in other situations, such as with grant providers, potential partners, senior staff and even suppliers. I have used business plans in the past, for instance, as a way of getting better credit from suppliers and banks.

Another point: I mentioned that you probably won't refer to your business plan once you are up and running. Of course, there is much to be said for updating your business plan every six to twelve months. In this respect your original could be the basis of a living document. 'It is a bad plan', said Publilius Syrus, the first-century Latin writer, 'that admits of no modification'. A business plan is, in some respects, a statement of intent, providing details of how you and your colleagues plan to develop your venture, who is going to do what and when, and how (you hope) the financial side of things will work out.

The Contents

It is your plan, so you can decide what to include in it. To my mind the most valuable elements are the executive summary and the figures. Indeed, I believe that the key financial projections are so important that they should be in the first paragraph of the summary.

I wouldn't waste a lot of time on the overall size of the market unless it is relevant. For example, if you are opening a shop it could be important to know what sort of passing trade you can expect. But if you are launching an online yoga mat business, you can probably take it as read that the market is vast. Below I summarise what I believe are the key elements of a business plan.

Executive Summary

Think of this as the 'elevator pitch'. In a few short paragraphs explain the finances and what your business is going to do. Include information about who your customers are, the opportunity you have identified and how you are going to satisfy it. You need to show that you have a way of attracting customers and also why those customers will be happy to pay for your goods or services. This is the place to describe your vision. You need to make the business sound exciting, unique and utterly irresistible to both customers and suppliers. Put proper emphasis on the investment required and the anticipated return. The executive summary is the most valuable part of the business plan, if only because most people you give it to will never read the rest of it. Indeed, the rest is really the work required to arrive at this summary.

The Opportunity and How You Are Going to Satisfy It

It's important to describe the opportunity in plain English. For instance, the opportunity may be that there are tens of millions of people in remote parts of Africa who have no access to electricity. You may be planning to satisfy their need by providing low-cost solar panels that they can pay for over, say, eighteen months via mobile phone banking. Describe your market and explain how large it is and whether it is growing or shrinking. Set out your unique proposition.

The Proof

If you have conducted a pilot or done some other research to show that this opportunity exists, explain what you did, what the results were and why the results show that the business will be a success.

Distribution and Payment

Explain how you plan to distribute your product or service, how customers are going to pay for it and what it is going to cost.

The Competition

Who are your competitors? What do they sell? Why will customers choose your products over theirs? Are there any barriers to entry (in other words anything that makes it hard to get into this market)? Do you face any threats?

Marketing

I have seen innumerable businesses fail because their promoters didn't have a good marketing plan in place. If you don't have an effective way to sell your product or service you are never going to succeed. I offer some basic advice on marketing in Chapter 31 and sales in Chapter 32. It isn't rocket science and you don't have to be professionally trained to design and execute a really effective marketing plan. But if there is one area I wouldn't leave to chance it is how you are going to bring in the customers.

The Operation

Depending on what sort of business you are aiming to establish you may want to describe its operation in some detail. Areas that should be covered include where the business will be located, what physical resources it will require, how it will make the product or provide the service (or both), number of employees, any timing issues and so forth. In short, the nuts and bolts.

The Team

This is where you describe your own work/life experience, and your team's work/life experience, and why it is relevant to the business. If you are fundraising, this is where a lot of investors will look first. They will want to know if you and your colleagues are up to the task in hand.

The Figures

To begin with, describe all your revenue streams (product sales, fees, commission, licensing, advertising and so forth) and your cost structure (rent, staff, materials, maintenance, insurance, etc.). Set out all your capital costs. Where you are making assumptions (and you will be) try to justify them.

Next explain how much money your business will make and – crucially – when you will start getting paid.

Finally, prepare some projections using a spreadsheet. You should show profit and loss, balance sheet and cash flow for whatever period seems relevant. You will probably need professional help with this task.

Exit Strategy

Whether or not you are planning to sell your business in the future, investors will want to know when and how they are going to get their money back as well as the level of return they can expect to make. You need to explain the exit strategy to your investors.

Don't Be Afraid to Ask for Help

There are some excellent books, websites and software programs designed to make preparing a business plan relatively painless. However, the thing I most recommend is getting help from someone with experience. The first place I would look for input is a professional adviser such as a start-up consultant or an accountant. Then I would ask successful entrepreneurs and maybe even investors for their comments. There's nothing like exposing your plan to external scrutiny to help you refine it. Also, if you don't like what they say you can ignore it. However, it is important not to bury your head in the sand by ignoring unpalatable truths that are pointed out to you.

My one proviso is do not send it to anyone you are really hoping will give you money until after you are certain that it is completely finished. A potential investor who reads a poorly written plan once might not look at it again. A good strategy might be to begin by showing the plan to investors you know are likely to reject it. That way you will obtain an independent opinion without damaging your chances of raising the money you need.

While You're in Planning Mode

While planning is uppermost in your mind there are a number of other issues that you might like to consider at the same time.

Legal Structure

At some point you are going to need to decide how your business is going to be structured from a legal perspective. Your basic choices are sole trader, partnership, company, a combination of partnership and company, or co-operative. If you are concerned about any potential liability, a company or a combination of company and partnership is best. A co-operative will give you least control. For most people the choice of structure is linked to tax issues and in this regard you should take professional advice before deciding. Tax doesn't seem to be that important when you aren't paying any, but when the profits are rolling in you may feel differently.

How to Reward Your Team but Maintain Control

There are situations where you might feel that you would like to reward your team (or maybe a family member) but you don't want to risk losing control of your venture. There are different ways to achieve this. For instance, if you are forming a partnership you can incorporate how decisions are to be made into the partnership agreement. If you are going to use a company as your legal structure, my advice is to issue two types of share. Holders of 'A' shares have a vote at meetings but receive no dividend. Holders of 'B' shares have no voting rights but can receive a dividend. If you hold on to all the 'A' shares you will maintain control but you won't make any money unless you also hold 'B' shares and a dividend is declared.

Regulation and Compliance

It is tedious, but every business has to deal with regulatory and compliance issues. When a business is small and new it may sometimes be able to get away with a certain amount of rule flouting. However, I wouldn't recommend it. It is much better to build compliance into your systems from day one and to get your staff and suppliers used to whatever it is they have to do rather than to try to graft it on later. It is also more ethical.

Insurance

Many new businesses forget that they will need insurance and are surprised by the cost. It is often worth joining a trade or professional association as many negotiate special policies and rates for their members.

There Is No Other Route to Success

Your business plan may only be a page or two of typing, but it is vital. As Pablo Picasso said, 'Our goals can only be reached through the vehicle of a plan, in which we must fervently believe, and upon which we must vigorously act. There is no other route to success.'

26

CREATIVE WAYS OF RAISING MONEY

Federico Alvarez, a 31-year-old resident of Montevideo, Uruguay, longed to go to Hollywood and make films. The problem was that he had no background in the industry, no experience and no contacts. So he made a five-minute video called *Panic Attack!* (it's about an alien invasion) and posted it on YouTube, where it went viral. A few weeks later he was in Los Angeles signing a deal with Ghost House Pictures to write and direct a sci-fi film. He had managed to leverage a $300 video into a $30 million Hollywood blockbuster.

Alvarez was lucky. But he was also astute. He came up with a creative way to get what he wanted and that is what this chapter is really about: using lateral thinking to raise money for a project that is important to you. It is based on my own experience in this area. I wanted to go into the oil business but didn't have the tens of millions of euros required to invest in storage facilities, delivery lorries or a chain of petrol stations. I came up with a possible solution to my problem and was able to test the concept for €3,749. When it was clear that the business had legs I found a way to develop it into a €100 million company using, for the most part, assets and money belonging to other businesses at no huge capital cost to myself.

It is my overriding belief that, if at all possible, it is much better to fund your business – especially in its early stages – yourself. I would actually suggest that if you can't fund it yourself, maybe it would be better to pursue a different idea. The benefits of self-funding are that it's quicker (raising money takes time), you won't have to deal with third parties (looking after lenders and/or investors takes energy) and it's cheaper (whether you borrow or sell shares in your venture it is going to cost you). On the other hand, I do recognise that there are situations where outside funding is the only way forward.

How Much Do You Really Need?

Before you even begin to consider where you will find the money you need, I would urge you to spend time trying to reduce your start-up costs. Look at every single item of expense and ask yourself whether you couldn't find a cheaper way of achieving the same result.

Where to Find Funding

Supplier Funding

When Vicky Marshall wanted to launch Honey's Real Dog Food, an artisanal dog food company, she needed a commercial kitchen and £100,000 worth of machinery. She searched the property listings until she found an abandoned fish-processing factory, which the landlord had left empty because it wasn't financially viable to refurbish it, and negotiated free rent for a year in exchange for paying the property taxes. Then she found a company that sold the machinery she wanted and talked them into letting her pay them, interest free, over three years, with a six-month payment holiday to help her get started.

It is surprising how helpful suppliers will be if you have a good idea, a good credit history and good references. They will want some sort of tangible assurance that it isn't going to go horribly wrong. Honey's occupied the fish-processing factory on 'bare licence', which meant that the landlord could evict them at any time. Their machinery supplier retained the right to remove the equipment if more than one payment was missed. If you can't fund your enterprise yourself, your next port of call should be your prospective suppliers.

Customer Funding

It is not unusual in the world of property to sell something that hasn't yet been built, or 'off plan'. The customer pays a hefty deposit in exchange for a fixed price and possibly an 'early bird' discount; the property company can use each advance sale as a way of leveraging additional funding. In the consultancy sector start-ups frequently ask their first clients to pay fees upfront so that the company has money to get off the ground. Manufacturers, especially of bespoke products such as furniture, can demand quite substantial advance payments before they begin work. In short, the practice of getting customers to fund a business is widespread. If you are looking for money to finance your venture, consider whether your customers or future customers might help.

Crowdfunding

Imagine complete strangers giving you money to start your business without expecting anything back. When Eric Migicovsky couldn't raise the money required to start manufacturing his smartwatch concept he turned to the internet. A couple of weeks later 68,928 total strangers had given him a staggering $10,266,844 to help him get his project up and running. This is by no means an isolated case; tens of thousands of projects a year are now being made possible through a process called crowdfunding.

Crowdfunding works like this. You put together a presentation – ideally including a video – and post it on an appropriate crowdfunding website. Members of that site look at your presentation and if they like what they see, offer to support your project, usually with a straightforward cash donation. Each site has different rules. For instance, some demand that you set a target sum and if you don't raise at least that amount you get nothing at all. Most allow you to reward your supporters with a gift. This makes these sites an excellent way to launch a new product. So, if you want to go into, say, the smartwatch business you could reward supporters with a watch. In this respect crowdfunding can be like pre-selling a product (or service) before it exists.

The crowdfunding concept was launched in 2003 by a company called ArtistShare, although there are now several dozen other options.

There's a skill in creating presentations that work on crowdfunding sites, and it's worth studying the businesses that have been successful to see how they managed it. There are crowdfunding sites for every type of venture and they are also an excellent place to search for new ideas.

Social Lending

Another internet-based way to raise money is social lending, which is also known as person-to-person lending or P2P. One of the many advantages offered by the internet is that it cuts out the middleman, meaning bigger profits for sellers and lower prices for buyers. Another is that it can bring together people who might otherwise never meet. What P2P lending does is harness these two benefits by matching lenders and borrowers. For the lenders it means an opportunity to earn much higher rates of interest than they could ever hope to receive by depositing their money in a bank or building society. For the borrowers it is a chance to pay a lower rate of interest, get funding they might otherwise find difficult to obtain and avoid the bother of dealing with a bank. The first social lending sites were primarily used by private borrowers but now there are sites that specialise in providing loans to small businesses. You will have to prepare a presentation and it is unlikely to work if you have a poor credit history.

Family, Friends and Other Contacts

I am not sure what percentage of businesses are funded by the founder's family, friends and other contacts but I am willing to bet it is a surprisingly high figure. For the sake of all concerned, formalise the arrangement; this avoids disagreement, uncertainty and resentment later on. You can find loan agreement templates online. Just make sure that whatever document you use includes how much is being borrowed, over what period of time and at what interest rate (if any). If there are to be regular repayments, explain how they are to be calculated and when they are to be made. The agreement should cover what happens in the event of default.

Free Money

As I have already mentioned, I am not a big fan of government funding or grants because I hate filling out the paperwork and it takes so long to process. On the other hand, if you are looking for cash it would be insanity not to see if your start-up is eligible.

Selling Equity

If you decide to raise some or all of the money you need by selling shares in your company, I only have one piece of advice to offer you: pick investors who share a common goal. Agreeing a price and getting the money is only the beginning of what could be an extremely long relationship. You will, in effect, be in partnership with your investors, with all that that implies. The key conflicts tend to be over providing additional funds, the way the business is being run, costs and – if the business is doing well – the speed with which it can be sold off to a third party. These don't seem like big issues when you want the money, but when your business (I almost wrote 'your baby', because that's how most entrepreneurs view their businesses) is up and running you may feel differently.

One of the things new entrepreneurs often worry about is how much equity to give away in a funding round. I strongly advise preparing well in advance. Get your business and marketing plan completed and make sure you know how much cash you will require and what return you hope to show on it. The more information you have, and the more solid that information is, the more money you can expect to raise and the less equity you can plan to give away. Valuation is always part art and part science. In terms of numbers, I would try not to part with more than 30 per cent. Remember, too, that valuation is only one element of the mix. Others relate to control and whether your investor can do anything else to help your business. Bear in mind, too, that raising money is a time-consuming business. Allow anything from three months to a year.

Borrowing from a Financial Institution

There are quite a few options, including:

- Personal loans
- Loans from micro-lenders
- Asset-backed loans (where the loan is secured against an asset such as property, shares or an insurance policy)
- Business loans
- Invoice discounting (sometimes called factoring)
- Leasing

… and variations of the above. By and large, financial institutions don't really like lending to start-ups unless there is a track record, security and/or cash being injected from some other source (your savings, for instance, or a third-party investor). Interest rates are usually higher for new businesses, too. If this is the route you decide to follow, allow plenty of time and try to opt for institutions that specialise in business banking – they are more likely to want to support you.

How to Impress an Investor or Lender

Over the years I have pitched all sorts of businesses to all sorts of investors and lenders, and I have found that the secret is to adjust your presentation to your audience. A private or angel investor, a venture capital firm, a company interested in a strategic holding (perhaps because your business will enhance their business in some way) and a bank will each have a different focus. Nevertheless, there are a few things you can do that are guaranteed to impress:

- Start something that is a real business with solid, long-term prospects, not just a vehicle designed to achieve a quick exit. All investors want to feel they are backing something that has the potential to make a big impact.
- Get other people to say how great you and/or your idea is. Nothing adds credibility more than third-party endorsements from professionals, academics and/or CEOs of successful businesses.

- Keep the detail to the accompanying documents. Your presentation should be emotive – a bit like a live commercial. Ask beforehand how much time you have and leave time for your audience to ask questions.
- Focus on cash flow. Every investor likes to know when cash will start to come in and how much of it there will be. Incidentally, make sure your figures are realistic. If you are showing dramatic growth you really need to explain how and why it is going to happen.
- Full disclosure. Don't hide anything that may be discovered later.
- Identify an enemy. Investors like competition – it shows that a market exists.
- If you are asked whether you see yourself running the company for ever, don't let them think you are a megalomaniac. Say that you want to create a successful business and if in the future you aren't the right person for the job you will happily pass the baton on to someone else.
- Under-promise and over-deliver.

27

The Partnership Dilemma

One of the most important decisions facing any entrepreneur is whether to go it alone or enter into a partnership. The answer will depend on a huge range of factors, including the people involved, the nature of the business and the timing. Either way, it can make the difference between success and failure and for this reason I have devoted a whole chapter to the question.

I feel at this point that I should declare my own philosophy, which is to have a foot in both camps. My contribution (such as it is) to any venture does not usually require my day-to-day involvement. If I am good at anything at all (which some might question) it is brand strategy, marketing and finance. Therefore I prefer to have a partner who is happy to look after the detail and run the business.

The Advantages of Going It Alone

If you have the skills and resources to own and run a business by yourself, without partners, you enjoy two powerful advantages. First, you will have total control. Companies often thrive under a strong leader and not having to spend time discussing every decision with a partner (or partners) has much to be said for it. Second, you won't have to share the rewards. Without any partners you can keep all the profits for yourself and you don't risk your business being upset as a result of disagreement.

Of course, it must also be said that without partners you will miss out on the input of someone who cares (or should care) about the business as much as you do. If you feel you need extra support, one option is to appoint a really good board of directors or advisers, but this is unlikely to be practical for a small start-up.

The Advantages of Having Partners

A partner with skills that complement your own – someone who can provide real expertise, experience and talent – will be of enormous value to your business. Two heads are, after all, better than one. The right partner, a partner who shares your own vision and commitment, will make it possible for you to accelerate growth. Running a business is more enjoyable, too, when shared. Partners can bring added credibility, funding and customers. When you want to go on holiday and/or in the event of some personal mishap, a partner can provide the practical support you need. The fact that the business won't be dependent on just one person makes it less vulnerable, too. Partners make businesses stronger.

Choosing a Partner

Even if you know your prospective partner or partners well and have already reached an oral agreement about working together, I would urge caution. Here are some questions it is sensible to ask yourself when choosing a partner:

- Are you compatible? I nearly suggest you ask yourself if there is chemistry, because in a way that is what it is. Do you approach problems in the same way? Do you have the same attitudes? Do you share the same values? Do you have the same vision for the business? As in any relationship it is vital that you can both communicate well. After all, one can get over even serious disagreements if one is able to talk. Partners who are hesitant, combative or dogmatic make it harder to succeed.

- Do you have the same goals? If one partner wants to build a business to sell and the other wants to create something to pass to his or her children there could be trouble ahead. Make sure you and your partner's vision of the future is the same.
- Is your partner honest? What sort of a reputation do they have? If you don't know your partner intimately I strongly advise a background check. At the same time, make sure that he or she is financially stable.
- How hard does your partner work? It is extremely frustrating being in partnership with someone who doesn't work as hard as you do. Of course, if your partner brings something else to the relationship you may not mind. But still …
- What is your partner's personal life like? When you get married you don't just marry one person, you marry that person's family, too. The same is true in a business partnership. Beware of a partner with a demanding spouse who interferes in the business. Also, if your partner is dealing with a lot of personal issues, consider whether this will have an impact on your business.
- Who is going to be the boss? Total equality in partnerships is as rare as it is in marriage. It happens, but usually one of the partners has a stronger personality.

Finally, ask yourself if your prospective partner respects you. If he or she doesn't look up to you and isn't grateful for what you bring to the partnership … it isn't really a partnership, is it?

Making Sure the Partnership Works

You are, naturally enough, in a hurry to get on with your business. However, unless you have known your prospective partner for a long time I don't advise rushing into anything. Spend as much time as possible together getting to know and understand each other. Embarrassing and awkward as it may be to end things before they have even begun, it is nonetheless better to do so than when you are legally bound to each other.

When you enter into a partnership (whether you are in a legal partnership or hold shares in the same company) you should have a professionally drawn up partnership agreement covering:

- A description of your roles and responsibilities
- How the shares in the business and the profits are to be divided
- Which partner, if any, has control and over what decisions
- What money, if any, each of you is investing in and/or lending to the business
- How any liabilities are to be divided
- What remuneration and expenses each of you is entitled to
- The volume of time each of you will work in the business in any given period
- What holidays each of you will be entitled to
- How any disagreements will be resolved
- What will happen if one or other of you wishes to leave the partnership or break it up
- Whether formal partnership meetings are to be held and, if so, when
- What happens to the partnership/business if one or other of you dies

With regard to the last, slightly morbid point, I would strongly recommend that the business puts life cover in place for all the partners. Many partnerships arrange things so that if one partner dies the insurance is sufficient to buy out his or her interest in the business.

'The poor man who enters into a partnership with one who is rich', said Plautus, the Roman playwright, 'makes a risky venture'. In fact, I think the reverse is true. If your partner isn't investing money in the business, he or she isn't going to have the same vested interest in its success.

28

The Extraordinary Benefits Associated with Failure

I f you are worried about your new venture failing, or if you are concerned that previous failures may render you unsuitable to be an entrepreneur – *stop worrying*. This short chapter explains why failure can actually be extremely positive.

The Benefits of Failure

I have backed more business ideas that have come to nothing than I care to think about. In fact, statistically, this isn't so surprising. Business angels generally expect two out of three start-ups to fail; and, of course, the ones that do survive achieve varying degrees of success.

Failure forces us to be more resilient; it pushes us to accept (and adapt to) change and encourages us to be more creative. Scientists say that because it stops us doing the same thing over and over again it results in a re-wiring of our brains. More than anything else, failure leads to new experiences and experiments. It is only through trial and error that any sort of progress can be made. All of the many failures I have experienced have led to something bigger and better. As Samuel Beckett said, 'Ever tried. Ever failed. No matter. Try again. Fail again. Fail better.'

The Risks Associated with Success

As a direct corollary to this there is an argument that too much success is actually quite risky. If you have never failed at anything, you have never been tested. And if you have never been tested then when you are faced with a serious challenge or problem you may find yourself unable to cope with it. People who succeed all the time learn much less and tend to become unimaginative, conservative and narcissistic. Dealing efficiently with failure is a sign that you have inner strength and imagination. Anyone who has met with difficulties and survived is automatically stronger and wiser.

One of the unexpected side effects of living in a meritocracy is that not only has society become obsessed with winning, but it is also trying to banish the concept of losing. On balance, I don't think this is a good development.

The Advantage of Recognising Failure

We are conditioned to believe that persistence pays off and that giving up on any activity is, somehow, ethically wrong. As a result, when a business doesn't work out most people react by denying it, selectively reinterpreting the facts or chasing their losses. In chasing their losses they may well throw good money after bad and/or take on unnecessary risks in a desperate attempt to improve their financial situation. A better course of action is to take one's emotions out of the equation.

The advantage of facing up to the unpalatable truth (i.e. that your beloved business idea is not going to work out) sooner rather than later is that it will stop you wasting time and money. Moreover, if you are brave enough to ask your partners, employees, investors, bankers, competitors and customers for their feedback, you should be able to avoid repeating the same mistake again. 'It is fine to celebrate success but it is more important to heed the lessons of failure,' as Bill Gates said.

How to Reduce the Cost of Failure

It is possible to reduce the impact of failing by avoiding projects with a large potential downside. This brings me back to a point I made in an earlier chapter. If you only invest as much money and time as you can readily afford – and if you cut your losses sooner rather than later – failure has less of a sting.

When a former colleague complained that he wasn't getting favourable responses to his job applications I pointed out to him that it doesn't matter how many times you are rejected as long as you get one 'yes'. It's the same with business. If your concept doesn't work out, naturally you are going to feel unhappy about it. But the silver lining is that you are now free to try something else. And one step closer to finding something that works.

29

THE GENTLE ART OF NEGOTIATION
(AND WHY IT IS SO IMPORTANT)

One of the most useful and practical skills that any entrepreneur can possess is the ability to negotiate effectively. Many people associate negotiation with conflict, but in fact it is really about dialogue and its purpose is to reach an understanding and/or resolve a point of difference and/or agree a course of action. Ultimately, negotiation is about the exchange of information, communication, compromise and meeting the needs of everyone involved. Entrepreneurs engage in a great deal of negotiation – with customers, clients, suppliers, landlords, employees, investors, lenders and even friends and family members. Its purpose is always to ensure the health and success of the business and, in this regard, the entrepreneur is rarely negotiating for personal gain.

As a general point, before you even begin, try to establish some common ground. For example, 'You've said that you would like to come and work for me, and I really want you to, so the only question is how we can work out a deal that is going to make both of us happy.'

Another good way to start is by having a general discussion about whatever you are negotiating over. If you are talking to a prospective employee you might say, 'What we need to agree is your salary, commission levels, hours of work, holidays, benefits and title', before asking if there is anything you have forgotten.

Do not be shy about following Lord Chandos's maxim: he believed that flattery is the infantry of negotiation and in my experience he was absolutely right.

The world is divided into those who expect to negotiate and those who don't. Either way, remember that it is your right to ask for better terms.

Some Tips for Successful Negotiating

- *The value of manners*: Provided you are polite, few people ever mind being asked for better terms. What really makes fruitful discussion difficult is anger, suspicion and confrontation. If things start to heat up, suggest postponing negotiations for a while. And try not to bear a grudge; even if you have every reason to dislike the person you are negotiating with, hide it for the sake of a better deal.
- *Do your homework*: Whatever it is you are negotiating, the more information you have about it, the better the outcome you can expect. Suppose you are negotiating to buy a piece of machinery. Draw up a list of all the different options along with the features you like and dislike about each one. Research prices and find out what is available second-hand. It pays to educate yourself.
- *Discover what is important to the other party*: One of the most useful things to establish in any negotiation (early on, if possible) is what really matters to the other party. It could be something obvious – such as price – or it could be something else, such as closing the deal quickly, being paid in cash or securing future business. Understanding the other party's position will strengthen your own. Social interaction is an excellent aid to negotiation as it offers opportunities to discover more about the other party.
- *Have a breakpoint in mind*: Whether you are negotiating about price or something more complicated, have your 'breakpoint' in mind before you sit down. This is the minimum (or maximum) you will accept to close the deal. If you pass the breakpoint, you should always walk away. Emotional responses have no place in successful negotiation. Incidentally, a good way to evaluate any proposed deal is to weigh it against your best option in the absence of a deal

– what is often called the 'best alternative to a negotiated agreement' or BATNA.

- *Just say no*: The less you care about making a purchase or closing a sale, the stronger your negotiating position. Never be afraid to say no. There will be other deals.

- *It doesn't matter whether you go first or last*: There is a perception that whoever names their conditions first is in a weaker position. Rubbish. If you enter the negotiation well prepared and have a breakpoint in mind it doesn't make any difference. Also, although negotiation lore has it that you should let the other side go first, an opening price (or position) will serve as a reference point or anchor that your counterpart – even if they are an expert in the field – will feel subconsciously that they must adhere to. When buying remember to start well below whatever your minimum terms are. Incidentally, an interesting approach is to start by presenting multiple equivalent simultaneous offers. This can have the effect of immediately opening up the discussion.

- *Small is beautiful*: It isn't easy if, like me, you are impetuous, but it generally pays to negotiate in tiny increments. Let's say you are buying something and the seller asks for €10,000 and you have a breakpoint of €8,000. Start by offering, say, €7,000 and go up in €100 increments. As the negotiation progresses, reduce the amounts involved. Why? This suggests that you are getting close to your breakpoint.

- *Line up your arguments*: As part of your preparation process, make a list of all your arguments for being given the terms you want. If you are arguing about price these might include your loyalty as a customer, future business prospects, the state of the market, what you can afford, the size of the order, the speed with which you will pay and so forth. You may also like to list off all the reasons why you have doubts about the deal. There's no harm in sowing a little uncertainty.

- *Open the negotiation out*: If you get stuck on an issue, put it to one side and discuss something else. Let's say you can't agree on salary. Instead, talk about holiday entitlements or expenses and come back to salary afterwards. It may be that the potential employee would be willing to forgo a higher salary in exchange for, say, being able to work a day at home every week. If the other party makes a proposal you wish to reject, come back with an alternative.

- *Take the lead*: There are various techniques that do help in a negotiation. One is to sound confident (which is always much easier if you have done your research). Another is to say nothing. People feel very awkward when there is a silence. Often, the other party will want to break what they perceive is a deadlock. This will almost definitely be to your advantage. You may also, if the conversation becomes heated, try speaking in a whisper. This has the effect of quietening people down and forcing them to listen.

- *If you are in a hurry*: It is best not to be in a hurry, but if you need a quick decision here is an approach that can be highly effective. Simply say to the other party, 'Let's not waste time. Name your best terms and if they're acceptable I will agree immediately without argument; if they're not I will walk away. But if I start to walk away and you come back to me with a better deal I will still say "no" as a matter of principle.' This tactic can work incredibly well, but only if the other party realises you are serious.

- Finally, try to *avoid inconsistency* in any negotiation. Time and again I have seen people leap around between different offers in a very disorganised way. This does not lead to a good outcome. Remember, your objective is not just to do the best possible deal for yourself, but to ensure that all parties to a deal are satisfied.

30

HOW TO BUILD A STRONG BUSINESS

The original Pony Express, founded in 1860, captured the world's imagination. The company set up a series of relay stations right across America so that mail could be delivered from east to west in as little as ten days. Its launch was greeted with fireworks and musical bands and its most famous courier, William Cody – better known as Buffalo Bill – became a legendary figure. However, the Pony Express closed eighteen months after it opened. During this period it had burned through $200,000 (the equivalent of $5.4 million today) of its investors' money without showing a profit. Why did it fail? The telegraph. Potential customers could see no reason to pay for a courier when they could get their message delivered in seconds for a fraction of the price. The extraordinary thing about this whole story is that the founders of the Pony Express knew all about the telegraph when they launched.

Some Basic Steps to Ensure that Your Business Succeeds

The Pony Express is the perfect example of how easy it is to get carried away with an idea, to put one's own and other people's money into it, but to fail to see its flaws. And recognising the flaws in your business plan – and rectifying them – is vital if your venture is to grow and prosper. Here are some basic steps you should take to ensure that the business you build is built to last.

- *Protect your credit*: You may not intend to borrow any time in the foreseeable future but it still makes sense to maintain a high credit rating just in case. Settle your bills on time and if you are having trouble making a payment, let the company or bank know why. If there is a dispute on a payment, get something in writing that says you aren't to blame.
- *Coddle your employees*: One happy, motivated and fulfilled employee is probably worth ten unhappy, despondent and frustrated employees – maybe more. If you can't reward your employees with above average salaries then show that they are appreciated in other ways. For example, send them cards or flowers, give them theatre or film tickets, treat them to lunch or even the occasional sandwich. Remember, too, that time off in lieu of extra salary is always appreciated.
- *Provide exceptional customer service*: Customer service is, generally speaking, so poor nowadays that when a company really makes an effort to excel it gets noticed. What's more, providing a genuinely personal, friendly and efficient service costs very little. Satisfied customers will not only keep coming back, but will also recommend you.
- *Run a tight ship – a very tight ship*: Do a line-by-line item check of your expenses every month. Cut whatever expenses you can. Be ruthless. Put any significant item or service out to tender on a regular basis. Every euro, dollar or pound you save is profit you don't have to earn.
- *Don't make knee-jerk decisions*: Our bodies often react to something before our minds have completely absorbed what is happening, for example when a driver swerves to avoid something before he or she has consciously recognised the danger. In the 1960s the neuroscientist Paul MacLean developed a theory that this is because part of the human brain had never really evolved (he referred to it as the reptilian brain) but, whatever the theory, it can cost you money. Unless you are planning a business that requires spur-of-the-moment, life-or-death decisions you have as much time as

you need to think every situation through. When someone says or does something that annoys or worries you, do not react. There's a place, of course, for spontaneous anger, but generally the accidental entrepreneur fares better if he or she doesn't make knee-jerk decisions. Also, there is no harm in saying to someone that you need time to think through your response. In fact, it is an excellent way to put you at a psychological advantage.

- *Delegate or die*: Delegation is a key management tool if a business is to grow and make money. Even if your employees aren't as effective as you, they still multiply your own effort. Look at it this way. Suppose you have five employees who are each only 80 per cent as efficient as you. Between them they will manage 400 per cent of your effort, something you could never achieve without them. Entrepreneurs who fail to grasp this basic formula rarely manage to expand their businesses.

- *Stay on top of the news*: Your business isn't operating in a vacuum. Stay on top of all the relevant industry news and, in particular, keep up to date on what your competition is doing. If they seem to be thriving, work out why. If they are not doing well, work out how to take advantage of the situation.

- *Review your pricing and other terms of trade*: Unless your business happens to be located in a country suffering from deflation, your costs are likely to be rising year on year. Make sure that your pricing keeps pace with your expenses. If you offer customers credit, check that it is worth your while. You are running a business, not a charity. When times get tough you need to let your late-paying or non-paying customers know that it is time for them to settle up regularly or look elsewhere.

- *Keep inventory to a minimum*: Keeping your inventory to a bare minimum will help you conserve cash. Never purchase more inventory than you can sell quickly. Negotiate with your suppliers to operate a just-in-time (JIT) ordering strategy, whereby you never have to carry stock. Consider whether you could actually get the product you are selling shipped direct from your suppliers to your customers. This is something that companies like Amazon have turned into a fine art.

- *Ask your customers for feedback*: Communicate regularly with your customers and ask them for lots of feedback. Use surveys, comment cards and one-to-one conversations to discover how you can better serve them.
- *Beef up your marketing*: No matter how fast your business is growing, marketing should always be a priority. As finding time to manage a really comprehensive communications strategy can be difficult, I recommend breaking it down into small, half-hour tasks and pledging to do one thing every day.
- *Work 'on', not 'in' the business*: Many entrepreneurs spend all their time doing tasks to keep their business going and forget to stand back and take a helicopter view. Make time to look at the bigger picture, and you will really grow your business.
- *Employ more women*: In 2012 Credit Suisse did some research into why some companies do better than others and they found that the secret was female brainpower. Tracking the performance of 2,400 businesses worldwide over a period of seven years, they discovered that the shares of companies whose boards included at least one woman outperformed those of companies with all-male boards – by 26 per cent! The trend really took off after the banking crisis in 2008, leading researchers to suggest that companies with female board members are succeeding because women are (perhaps) more risk averse or, rather, that they plan more carefully before making any major decision.
- *Don't ignore the legal stuff*: It is only too easy to put off all sorts of boring tasks – such as legal paperwork – when you are busy running a business. The consequences may be more serious than you imagine. When I was selling my €100 million business, GreatGas, the shareholder register and all the other documentation hadn't been properly completed by the firm assigned to do it. Their oversight, and my failure to spot it, could easily have scuppered the deal. Don't forget, either, to apply for relevant patents and trademarks.

Why New Business Isn't Everything

It is well said that your existing customer may be your best customer. It should cost you less time and money to make an additional sale because you already have a relationship and for the customer there is the advantage of convenience. How can you persuade existing customers to buy more from you and/or to buy more frequently? The first step is to track customer retention (the average time a customer remains active) and customer value (the average amount each customer is worth). Armed with this information you can try different approaches and offers to improve your performance.

Is it better to have a small number of really big spending customers, or a big number of much lower spending customers? It depends what business you are in, of course. It is true that customers with more money to spend tend to be better credit risks, but against this:

- They could suddenly take their business elsewhere, leaving you high and dry.
- If they know you are dependent on them they may let you gear up to handle their business and then force you to drop your prices, wiping out your profit.
- In order to keep them happy you may have to change how you work in ways you don't really like.
- If your contact(s) in the organisation leave, you could lose the business.

My own preference is for building more diverse businesses that depend on the many rather than the few. I believe that having a large customer base makes you less vulnerable: if you lose a customer here or there it may make you unhappy, but it won't be a crushing blow.

Be Prepared to Manage Growth

Rapid growth kills off as many businesses as no growth at all. So if you are fortunate enough to be managing a rapidly expanding business, what should you look out for and how should you deal with it?

- *Square pegs/round holes*: It is better, for both the business and the individual, to face up to underperforming staff. The best initial solution is retraining, as it is far less expensive to continue to work with existing staff than to recruit new, untrained staff. The bottom line though is that if you have a square peg in a round hole you need to face up to the difficult task of removing the person from the workforce as soon as possible, within your local labour laws.

- *Staff numbers*: It takes time to recruit and time to train good staff, particularly if their role includes customer service. My advice is to bring on staff before you need them so that they can absorb your culture and shadow existing members of staff. Of course, it is more expensive in the short term, but should more than pay dividends in the long term.

- *System failures*: By 'systems' I mean the way in which the core functions of your business are organised. These include not just the design, manufacture and distribution of your products or services, but also accounting, human resources, technology and security. Good systems will save you money and are worth investing in sooner rather than later.

- *Cash and capacity shortages*: Fast-growing businesses have a habit of sucking up cash. Rapidly expanding sales means rapidly expanding costs. Plan ahead and make sure you have enough cash before you need it. At the same time make sure you have the capacity to deal with sales.

How to Keep Your Customers Loyal

Lasting, authentic relationships can only help a business grow and prosper. For an entrepreneur the most important of these relationships is with his or her customers. Take away the customers, after all, and what have you got? Here are a few tips on how to engender such relationships and make them last.

- *Keep in touch*: It is often a case of 'out of sight, out of mind'; if your customers don't hear from you regularly they may quickly forget you. Establish a system for contacting customers on a regular basis.

Don't inundate them, obviously, and gear the frequency of your contact to the nature of your business. Remember, there are lots of ways to stay in touch with customers, including email, social media, telephone, mailings and face-to-face meetings. Even if customers don't attend, they will appreciate being invited to special events and it is an excellent method of building your customer relationship.

- *Make it personal*: If you run a small business with a small number of customers you can contact them yourself – by phone, email or in person. If you have a larger business you can still make the contact personal by writing the message yourself and making sure that your customers have a way of getting directly in touch with you. At an absolute minimum, send out a quarterly newsletter.

- *Be self-aware*: Do you welcome or avoid conflict? Do you tend to spend a long time thinking something through or do you make quick decisions? Are you more likely to consider every purchase carefully or to spend a little recklessly? There's no right or wrong answer to any of these questions and I raise them only to make the point that when you start your own business it is a good idea to be self-aware. You need to know your strengths and weaknesses and to assess how you will react to the different situations you are likely to encounter. More than this, running a business means contact with many other people: customers, suppliers and employees. If you don't understand yourself, you will be at a disadvantage when dealing with everyone else.

- *Think big*: I cannot overemphasise the value of thinking big. I am not suggesting that you set unrealistic goals, but that you consider yourself and what you are doing in a positive light. For example, supposing you are a bricklayer. You can view yourself simply as someone who lays bricks or as someone who is, say, building a cathedral. You are much more likely to succeed as an entrepreneur – accidental or otherwise – if you perceive what you are doing in this optimistic way. Indeed, there is plenty of scientific evidence that optimistic people achieve more and even enjoy better health. The Mayo Clinic conducted research that revealed a number of health benefits associated with optimism, including a reduced risk of death from cardiovascular problems, less depression and an increased lifespan.

- *Learn to improve other people's performance*: In the late 1960s two researchers, Robert Rosenthal and Lenore Jacobson, discovered that if teachers are led to expect enhanced performance from some children, those children do, in fact, perform better (the Pygmalion effect). In 1979 Robert Feldman and Thomas Prohaska discovered that the reverse is also true and that low expectations lead to poorer performance. Knowing that there is a direct correlation between perception and performance is of enormous value to accidental entrepreneurs. If we expect more from our suppliers and employees, we will get more. Better still, we don't necessarily have to expect more, we just have to persuade whoever we are dealing with that we do. (By the same token, if one wants to kill a project without upsetting people, simply planting the idea that it won't work may be enough to convince them.)
- *Use case histories and testimonials*: One of the best ways of retaining customers and boosting customer loyalty is to provide them with case histories and testimonials. It is a good reminder of what you do and an ideal way to highlight the key services and benefits you offer. People remember real stories, too, in a way they never remember sales copy.
- *Reward them for introducing business to you*: If a customer recommends you to a third party, acknowledge it with a special card or letter and, ideally, an appropriate gift.
- *Offer loyalty gifts and bonuses*: Make your customers feel special by rewarding them with extra benefits, free products or services. Consider launching a formal loyalty programme.

31

THE PERFECT MARKETING PLAN

The first business plan for my €100 million company, GreatGas, consisted of a short 'to do' list and a page of financial calculations. The marketing plan, on the other hand, was much more detailed and ran to page after page of ideas, research, costs and copy. Why so much emphasis on marketing compared to the rest of the venture? You can have the most brilliant idea in the world, but if you don't market it correctly the chances of it coming to anything are very slim.

If you find the thought of producing a marketing plan a little daunting, bear in mind that marketing is nothing more than the art (and very occasionally the science) of communicating information. In fact, I wish it were called 'communicating' instead of 'marketing' because then perhaps more people would realise how straightforward a discipline it is. I am not saying it doesn't help to have a bit of a flair for the subject, but really it isn't terribly complicated and whether you intend to employ outside experts or handle everything yourself, this short chapter should help you to formulate an effective marketing plan.

First Things First

Shortly after I started working in the Bank of Ireland marketing department over thirty years ago, one of my advisers explained to me that everything I would be required to do could, broadly speaking, be divided into one or more of the following activities:

- *Advertising*: You pay someone else (such as a newspaper or television or radio station) to communicate your message for you.
- *Direct response*: Your advertising is designed to achieve a measurable response, such as someone placing an order or telephoning for more information.
- *Public relations (PR)*: You try to get someone else, invariably a journalist, to communicate your message for you. It can also include other activities (such as events) that will present your business to your audience in a favourable light.
- *Sales promotion*: You encourage your audience to make a purchase by offering them an incentive.
- *Packaging, print and design*: You use your product packaging, printed material and design to communicate your message.

In one sense not much has changed and I still use the above as a checklist when planning any marketing activity. Indeed, the only real difference between then and now is the range of media options. Here is a simplified list of all the main places you can market your business:

- *Broadcast media*: television and radio commercials
- *Print media*: newspapers, magazines, direct mailings, newsletters, etc.
- *Outdoor media*: billboards, posters, signage, etc.
- *Digital media*: websites, social media (e.g. Facebook, Twitter, blogs), email, SMS, etc.
- *Experiential media*: events, trade shows, exhibitions and other one-to-one encounters that are related to an actual experience
- *Alternative media*: everything from display stands in supermarkets to the back of car-park tickets

A well-written marketing plan will identify the most appropriate activities and the most appropriate media.

The Four Ps (aka the Marketing Mix)

When you come to plan your marketing activity it can be helpful to refer to something known as the four Ps (also called the marketing mix), which was invented by a marketing genius called Edmund Jerome McCarthy in the 1960s and is still relevant today. The four Ps are:

- *Product*: It is important to have the right product or service for your market.
- *Price*: You need to sell your product or service at a price that makes your customers feel that they are getting value.
- *Promotion*: What you are going to tell your customers and via which media.
- *Place*: Distributing your product or service in such a way as to make it easy for your customers to find it.

The overall objective of most marketing strategies is to put the right product at the right price in the right place and to promote it in the right way.

What Goes into a Marketing Plan?

An effective marketing plan will contain most of the following elements.

Overview

This is really an explanation of what the product or service is, its benefits, who it's aimed at, whether there is any competition and – broadly speaking – how it will be brought to market. Explain what distinguishes your product from the competition and how it will be distributed. Describe any other relevant factors, for example if there are time constraints that will affect the marketing.

Objectives

Your specific objectives will be determined largely by the method of distribution. For example, if you are selling a product direct to the public via a website, your objectives might be to (a) generate visits to the site, (b) convert site visitors to customers, (c) generate repeat visits and sales, (d) increase the value of each sale and (e) encourage customers to recommend you to their friends and relations. Marketing objectives generally include generating sales leads, converting sales leads and increasing customer value. Some businesses use advertising/marketing to create the right image for their business. This is called awareness marketing.

Targets

Set your targets. How many leads do you want? What percentage of leads do you expect to convert to customers? How much will those customers spend with you? How often do you expect them to return and buy more? How long do you expect them to remain active customers?

The Market

Describe your customers. If you don't know much about them, do some research (see below). Set out who they are, what they like and dislike and – crucially – what they need. In some cases you may be targeting a niche market. For instance, if you are going to produce gluten-free flour you know that your market will be coeliacs (and their family members). In other cases, your market may be much larger. For instance, if you are going to manufacture toilet paper made from recycled pulp you know that your market is almost every home and business in the country. Of course, the size and nature of the market is only part of the story. Your product may be of much greater interest to a certain segment of the market. In the case of coeliacs, this segment might be people who bake; in the case of toilet paper buyers it could be those with an interest in the environment.

The Competition

There's always plenty to be learned from your competition and I recommend studying their products, pricing and marketing even if you plan to do something completely different.

Tactics

Describe your tactics. Start with distribution. How are you going to sell your product or service? The main options are via a third party (such as a wholesaler, retailer or dealer), direct (for example through a website) and/or using a sales force (these may be employed, on commission or part of a multi-level marketing network). You could also sell via franchisees. Next, consider where you are going to sell your product or service. If you have a shop your market will be limited to those within easy reach, whereas if you are in manufacturing you may be able to sell all over the world.

Pricing and Offers

Set out your pricing policy. This isn't simply a matter of setting a price; it's about creating a package that will attract customers. When Netflix started they were in the business of renting out films and television programmes on DVD (they have since slightly changed their business model). Unlike other providers (basically bricks and mortar 'video' shops), Netflix charged a flat subscription for unlimited rentals and didn't impose a late return fee. Another broader-based example is the companies that manufacture computer printers, which generally sell them at cost or even at a loss. This is because they make their real profits by selling branded ink cartridges, on which there is a stupendous mark-up.

It is generally a good idea to test different prices and offers.

Message

What do you want to tell your market? Make a list of all the messages and prioritise them. When TOMS launched, their main message was simple: for every pair of shoes sold the company would give a free pair of shoes to someone who needed them. There were also secondary messages to do with the design and manufacture of the shoes, the company's ethical stance and so forth.

Media

Having established who you want to reach and what you want to say to them, you need to decide the best media to reach them. When I was launching GreatGas, my target market was the owners of independent fuel stations in Ireland. There were fewer than 2,000 decision makers with whom I wanted to communicate. So my chosen media were mail, telephone, trade advertising and trade exhibitions.

Campaign Plan

This is perhaps the most imaginative part of writing a marketing plan. You need to work out what you are going to do and when. Each campaign should have a clear objective, target audience and readily understandable activity. You should also cost the campaign and draw up an action list of the things you need to do to make it happen.

A word of caution: make sure each campaign is relevant. It is easy to get carried away with activities that are entertaining but not cost effective. It is impossible to list off all the different campaigns you might want to run, but here are some simple ideas to get your own creative juices flowing:

- Build a website
- Buy a list of prospects and send them a printed mailing piece
- Run an advertisement in appropriate newspapers and magazines
- Run banner ads on other businesses' websites
- Telephone your prospects
- Email your prospects
- Run a free draw or competition to gather names for future campaigns
- Start a blog
- Set up a Facebook page
- Create some videos and post them on Vimeo or YouTube
- Improve your online presence through search engine optimisation (SEO)

- Organise a seminar and invite your prospects
- Issue a press release
- Write some articles and send them to appropriate media
- Hold a party
- Rent a stand at an exhibition or show
- Hand out free samples of your product
- Distribute leaflets on the street
- Deliver a leaflet to homes and/or businesses in your area
- Hold a launch event
- SMS your prospects
- Run some TV or radio commercials
- Arrange a stunt
- Put up posters
- Produce some podcasts
- Develop a free smartphone app
- Give away free merchandise (pens, mugs, shopping bags, etc.)
- Organise a pop-up shop
- Distribute money-off vouchers
- Produce a newsletter and give or send it to prospects and customers

If you see a campaign you like, make a note of it. There is nothing wrong with copying and adapting other people's ideas.

Budget

Cost every part of your marketing plan.

Timing

Create a rolling calendar for your marketing plan so that you always know what is coming up in the future. You should also consider timing your marketing to coincide with particular times of the year, such as New Year for any fitness or diet products or services, or late summer/back-to-school time for products aimed at students and parents.

Monitor

You should aim to regularly monitor the results of your marketing to ascertain which elements of your strategy are working and/or if you should rethink your approach.

The Importance of Creating a Brand

One of the first things you need to do as part of your marketing strategy is to create a brand for your business. By 'brand' I mean a single, consistent visual, verbal and written message describing your business. I would actually recommend creating a manual that explains your brand in words and pictures. In it you could include:

- The company logo and colours and how they are to be applied to everything from stationery to signage
- Your core values, which might include your pricing policy, ethical beliefs, how you will treat customers, environmental policy and so on
- What makes your business different
- What is important to you
- How you intend to communicate your message to your customers and prospective customers

The best brands are emotive and offer authenticity, integrity and honesty. They reflect the aspirations and interests of their customers.

The Importance of Buzz

In the 1990s an unusual thing happened to the shoe brand Hush Puppies. Sales had dropped to such an extent that Wolverine, the manufacturer, was considering dumping the line altogether. Then something occurred that was nothing less than marketing magic. A shoe that was considered (if you will excuse the pun) a dog suddenly became a fashion hound. As Malcolm Gladwell, author of *The Tipping Point*, explains:

At a fashion shoot two Hush Puppy executives – Owen Baxter and Jeffery Lewis – ran into a stylist from New York who told them that the classic Hush Puppies had suddenly become hip in the clubs and bars of downtown Manhattan.

Hush Puppies had been the lucky recipient of 'buzz'. *Newsweek* describes buzz as '[i]nfectious chatter; genuine, street level excitement about a hot new person, place or thing.' You could also describe it as old-fashioned word-of-mouth endorsement. There's no way of guaranteeing that your company will get talked up like this, but you can do things to increase your chances:

- *Make your business human*: Don't be stuffy or impose rules or conditions that aren't really necessary.
- *Keep a sense of humour*: Customers warm to companies that make them laugh because most businesses take themselves very seriously.
- *Be authentic*: Customers also respond well to authenticity.
- *Be original*: Thinking outside the box often helps to create buzz.
- *Resist the trend*: Being different will mark you out and generate extra interest in what you offer.

Once there's a bit of buzz about your brand it can last for years. Creating a buzz does not necessarily cost a great deal. A good example of inexpensive buzz was the Ballymaloe Space Project. In order to show off what they were capable of, a young creative agency announced Ireland's first space programme. The team sent a jar of Ballymaloe Country Relish into space (and brought it back again) at a cost of around €700. They attracted international media attention for both themselves and Ballymaloe Country Relish.

The Importance of Competitive Intelligence

Competitive intelligence is exactly what it sounds like. It involves finding out what your business competitors are up to and can include such information as their cost base, sales, profitability, staffing policy, marketing strategy and supplier details. Knowing what is and isn't working for your competitors will help you formulate your own strategy.

A good way to start a competitive intelligence programme is to draw up a list of, say, ten of your closest competitors. If you aren't sure which companies to investigate you can always ask your customers for suggestions. Once you have the list, do some basic desk research: look at their websites, their online presence, what their customers are saying about them and anything else you can find out without leaving home. Telephone them pretending to be a customer and see how they operate. You could also write or telephone to ask for copies of their literature and look at their annual report and accounts.

Once you have a feel for the company, move to the field research stage. Visit their premises and see what you can learn just from wandering around and talking to their staff and customers. If there is information you would specifically like you may be able to obtain it by simply asking.

Next do a little experiential research. Try out their products and services for yourself. Evaluate the experience. Discover how they look after their customers.

How to Conduct Inexpensive Research

Larger companies can afford to call in professional researchers, but if you run a small to medium-sized business such a luxury is unlikely to be open to you. Instead, I suggest starting your research programme by asking yourself a series of probing questions, such as:

- How large is the potential market?
- Why is now a good time to launch?
- What is the product or service replacing?
- Will people repeat purchase?
- What improvements could I make to the product or service?
- Who is my competition and what are they doing that is (and is not) working?

Remember, there are lots and lots of easy ways to test your idea before you invest in setting up your business. Here are some of the different ways you can research your concept:

1. *Ask friends*: The candid opinion of a reliable friend can save you a great deal of effort and money.
2. *Ask potential customers*: Show them prototypes, mock-ups, drawings and anything else that will give them a feel for what you propose.
3. *Advertise*: Run an advertisement to attract enquiries. This is an inexpensive way to see what sort of response you are likely to get.
4. *Seek editorials*: Your new idea may well be newsworthy. Ask editors of publications your customers read to profile you and your concept to see if it stimulates comment and perhaps enquiries.
5. *Offer advertising agencies a chance to pitch for your business*: Their questions, comments and ideas will help you shape your thinking.
6. *Run street surveys*: Literally stop people in the street and solicit their views.
7. *Run focus groups*: Pull together a group of potential customers and ask them to give their opinion on whatever it is you are planning.
8. *Look for academic and other research*.

What Should You Say in Your Communications?

Whatever marketing you plan there is going to come a moment when you will have to decide what to say to your prospects. There is so much advice available on this subject that I am not going to repeat it all here. I do want to make a few general observations, however.

In my experience the best place to start is to write down – in two columns – all the product's features and benefits. Remember, features are descriptive (for instance, low-energy light bulbs) and benefits are emotional (they last longer, save money and are better for the environment). Rank the list.

Next, consider any offer you want to make ('buy one get one free'), any time restrictions ('buy now before the VAT increase') and any other factors you may want to mention (what your competitors are doing). Finally, pull it all together into a single page and use this as your briefing document.

If you don't have the time or inclination to write your own copy I would strongly recommend getting in professional support. A good copywriter will be able to produce whatever material you need to communicate your core messages and values not just to your customers but also to staff and suppliers.

32

HOW TO SUCCEED WITHOUT SELLING

If, like me, you are not a natural salesperson, you should find what follows of great interest. (If you are a natural salesperson read on anyway, as you may just pick up a few tips.) This chapter is all about how to achieve business success without having to hard sell.

There are people capable of persuading anyone to buy anything, whether they need it or not, for more than they ever meant to pay. These sales are achieved, as far as one can tell, through a combination of persistence, charisma and confidence. I am not saying such über-salesmen don't do their research or are necessarily unscrupulous, more that they are fortunate enough to possess an innate talent for selling, together with a comprehensive understanding of all the different techniques that can be employed to convince someone to buy.

The main reason why I shy away from selling is that I don't like being pushy. Moreover, I find that although I have no trouble understanding sales theory, when it comes to putting it into practice everything I have learned flies straight out of the window. The underlying problem is that, for personal reasons, I want my customers and clients to make their purchasing decisions by themselves, based on hard evidence and not because I have attempted to 'hard sell' them. However, I never have a problem when I am selling a product or service in which I really believe.

Yet, despite (or, to be more accurate, because of) my dislike for anything that might be described as hard selling, I have developed an eccentric but effective way to tackle the whole sales process. It is incredibly simple; you'll master it in a matter of minutes; and, with one proviso, it works. The proviso? It is of no possible use if you are trying to sell something inappropriate to someone who doesn't really need it. On the other hand, if you have a product or service that offers genuine benefits, my low-key, accidental approach to selling will deliver solid results.

Put Yourself in the Customer's Shoes

If you understand what your prospective customer's priorities are, you will be able to work out whether the product or service you are offering meets their needs and, if so, to what extent. The first step to achieving this is to gather information. Begin by asking your customer questions. What are you looking for? Why? When for? What features do you require? What budget do you have? If you don't have a budget, what price range are you thinking of? Obviously, you don't want to subject your prospect to a modern-day version of the Spanish Inquisition. On the other hand, you shouldn't interrupt too much, either. The real secret is to listen.

Sadly, many salespeople seem to lack listening skills. Instead they talk about themselves and what they know. Enthusiasm is good, of course, but chatting away in the hope that something you say will strike a chord and lead to a sale is likely to be self-defeating. In order to emphasise that I am listening, I often ask customers if they mind me taking notes. Apart from being useful, this reinforces the idea that I believe whoever I am talking to has something important to say. I also encourage my prospect to give me lots of detail. Incidentally, if you find it difficult to get someone to open up you could try parroting – repeating the customer's last few words as a question to get them to elaborate on the topic. For example, if the customer says, 'It was going really well until we encountered the penguin problem', your response would be, 'Tell me about the penguins.' Another good idea is to provide your customer with an occasional summary of what they have been saying to demonstrate that you have been paying attention.

Generate More Leads than You Need

I suspect that one of the reasons why many salespeople are pushy is that they are short of leads. If, on the other hand, you have more inquiries than you can reasonably deal with, the pressure to sell completely disappears. Instead, you can focus on providing the best possible advice and even, when appropriate, recommend your competitors.

Finding Your First Customers

Before you can start looking for new business you need to have a clear picture of your perfect customer. Here are some questions that will help you:

- Are your customers individuals, businesses or some other sort of organisation?
- Where are they located?
- Who makes the decision to buy?
- What sort of income do they have?
- To what extent is this a discretionary purchase?
- What motivates the purchase?
- How old are your typical customers?
- Are your customers primarily male or female?
- Do they shop around before making a buying decision?
- What is important to them?
- How long does it take them to make a decision?

Once you have defined your customer you can start working out where to find them:

- Could you buy or rent a list of prospects? If you can, consider contacting them via telephone, SMS, email or direct mail.
- What specialist media (newspapers, magazines, websites, etc.) do they read? Can you get free coverage and/or advertise?
- Do you have any personal contacts (friends, relatives, neighbours or colleagues) you could approach? Who might recommend you?

- Are there any trade organisations, clubs or associations you could join that would bring you into contact with possible customers?
- Are there any trade shows and exhibitions worth attending?
- Could you establish yourself as an expert by writing free of charge for websites, papers and trade publications? (If this is a possibility, focus on providing useful information, not making a blatant sales pitch.)
- Could you be talking to your competitors? You never know, they may give you referrals and, anyway, it is useful when speaking with prospects to have first-hand knowledge of the marketplace.
- Can you ask existing customers for referrals?
- Do you always have a business card and/or brochure on you? You never know who you are going to meet.
- Are you reading enough? Reading newspapers, trade magazines, advertising and websites is a great way to find leads.
- Could you make some news? Get to know the journalists who write for your market and feed them stories about your business.

Things to Do Instead of Selling

I may never push a sale or bother a customer or prospect, but that doesn't mean I am idle. Here are some of the non-selling things I recommend to support your sales process:

- *Stay match fit*: There is no doubt in my mind that if you are physically fit and rested you achieve much more than if you are in poor health and exhausted. A good diet, regular exercise and plenty of sleep will help you grow your business. If you find yourself getting stressed, I really recommend learning a simple meditation technique. I know it's common sense, but I need to constantly remind myself that there is a direct connection between overall health and performance.
- *Ask questions*: If you don't understand something, ask questions. You can do this without looking stupid. For instance, ask someone to explain what they said in more detail rather than just blurting

out what you think they said, which might make you look dim. Just think carefully first about how you will phrase the question.

- *Offer outstanding service*: One of my best friends, John Lowe, the Money Doctor, always completes as much of the paperwork as he can for his clients in advance of any meeting. That way they never have to fill out tedious forms. He is proactive, too, and often writes to tell them how they can save money by switching to a different provider. It is the little things like this that can make a difference. Stay in touch with your customers, not to get new business, but to see what you can do for them. You can't go wrong when customers tell you what they need and you deliver.
- *Know what makes you different*: List off three or four things that makes your business stand out from the competition. Keep them in the forefront of your mind so that you can remind your customers at the relevant time.
- *Be polite*: Good manners pay. Thank prospects for their time and interest even if they don't become customers. Remember, too, to ask customers about their experience of dealing with your business and really listen and respond to what they say.
- *Provide value*: There are people who make a purchasing decision solely on price. But anyone with a modicum of intelligence knows that price is only part of the equation. It is the quality of the product, the service standards, the after-sales care, and so forth that make the real difference. Don't focus on price; focus on value.
- *Offer samples and trials*: A good product or service speaks for itself. If possible, try to give your prospects an opportunity to try you out free of charge or at a reduced price. Experiencing what you do is worth hours of discussion!
- *Collect testimonials*: Ask satisfied customers for testimonials. Testimonials come in handy when prospects are on the fence about making a decision and they will often encourage your prospects to make up their mind.
- *Don't worry if nothing happens*: Henry Ford once said, 'Failure is simply the opportunity to begin again, this time more intelligently.' If you don't make a sale, don't worry. The crucial thing is that you

always leave a good impression with anyone you speak to. The rest will follow.

Using the Telephone

It is natural for anyone of a sensitive nature to be concerned about inflicting their company – even by telephone – on anyone else. As a result they develop a fear of cold calling. And yet, it is only cold calling if you are calling the wrong person on the wrong subject at the wrong time.

I collect bronze sculpture. If someone telephones me – day or night – with information about a sculpture I may be interested in, I will welcome the call. I have more than one mobile telephone. If someone telephones to tell me how I can reduce my bills (and I only wish someone would), provided they call at the right moment and say the right thing, I will also welcome the call. It is only when a call is irrelevant or intrusive that I resent it. So, in principle, there is no reason to avoid the telephone, even if you have never met the person you are calling. Here are some tips for calling customers and prospects:

- Have a clear objective. For instance, your objective might be a meeting.
- Don't think of them as sales calls. Think of them as research or introductory calls.
- Phone prospecting takes longer to pay off than other marketing efforts. Expect it to take some time to get results.
- Make sure you are calling the right person.
- Always start by explaining who you are, why you are calling and asking whether it is convenient to talk.
- Have a set of notes to work from, but try not to use a script.
- Get the 'gatekeepers' (secretaries, receptionists and switchboard operators) on side. They will help you find the person you really want to speak to.

Create the Right Tools

It is a great deal easier to explain to prospects what you do and why you do it so well if you have the right tools for the job. These might include leaflets, fact sheets, photographs, samples, models, videos, presentations, posters or any number of other options.

33

MONEY, MONEY, MONEY

There is an inordinate amount to do in the first year or two of launching a business and if maths isn't your forte you may be tempted to avoid thinking about it. Here are a few tips designed to help you master your finances.

Cash Is King

Cash, new entrepreneurs are told, is king, and this is true. It doesn't matter how profitable your business is, running out of cash may put all you have achieved at risk. The secret is to budget. I usually budget on a twelve-month rolling basis, with a secondary budget covering three to five years. Remember, a budget isn't about profit and loss; it is about your monthly inflows and expenditure. When you start up, you will need to make some assumptions before you can produce a budget. Below are the main issues to address.

Income

What will your income be for every month over the next twelve months? Over the next 36 to 60 months? To arrive at this figure you will also need to consider all your different potential sources of income as well as pricing and margins. Income is not the same as sales. Occasionally, income will come before you supply your goods or services, but generally it will come afterwards – often a long time afterwards. What payment terms will you offer customers if you sell on credit? How quickly will they pay?

Expenditure

Bear in mind that in the same way that income may trail behind your sales, expenditure may precede your income. So, when budgeting your expenditure, you will have to do more than work out what it will cost to supply the goods or services. You will need to think about inventory, operating expenses and staffing costs as well as all your overheads. What payment terms will your suppliers give you? How much will you need to borrow?

Capital Expenditure

What equipment will be needed to start the business? How much will it cost? Will there be additional equipment needs in subsequent years? How are you going to fund this and what will the funding cost? Profit is not cash, as you will find out very quickly if you are in a business that requires regular capital investment.

Sunk Costs

Management accountants use the term 'sunk cost' to refer to money that has already been spent and which can't be recovered. It's important to understand the concept because there may come a time when you are tempted to carry on investing time and cash in a business or project even though it is extremely unlikely to succeed. Under these circumstances it is vital to remember that there is (and this isn't something that you hear often enough from accountants) no point in throwing good money after bad.

How to Overcome Cash Flow Problems

When I said earlier that cash is king, what I should have said is that cash is *emperor*. This is especially the case during periods of economic instability when credit and equity funding may be difficult to find, no matter how well you are doing. Here is some hard-won advice on what to do if you see a cash flow crisis looming:

- Look hard – very hard – at your costs. Better to make cuts too early than too late.
- Prepare a weekly cash flow projection for the next twelve months detailing what income you have coming in and what bills you are going to pay.
- Stay in touch with your creditors. Visit them if it is convenient. If you are going to be late with a payment, let them know ahead of time. If you agree a payment plan make sure it is feasible and stick to it in order to re-establish your credibility. Creditors would rather have a part-payment than nothing. Show your creditors how you are planning to get out of the problem.
- Stay in even closer touch with your debtors. If the owner of a business calls looking for money, he or she usually receives better treatment than when 'someone in accounts' is chasing for payment.
- Try to switch capital expenditure to a lease basis. If you own your building, consider selling it and leasing it back.

You could also consider factoring (otherwise known as invoice discounting) your invoices. Factoring, in which financial institutions buy receivables (in other words, your unpaid invoices) for a discount and then take over the collection, is something large companies embrace more readily than small ones. It is just another form of financing. However, although it works well when a business is expanding, it can lead to cash flow problems if your turnover begins to fall and so I consider it a last resort.

Monitor Your Key Indicators

Once you pass your start-up stage and begin to have some trading history, one of the best ways to ensure that your business is on track is to analyse all your financial figures. Here are the key indicators you should monitor:

- *How many sales leads you are generating for the business.*
- *Your conversion or close rate:* This is the percentage of leads that convert into sales and it indicates the efficiency of your sales force and the quality of your leads. A low conversion rate is a sign that your sales force is not working effectively or that your leads are not sufficiently qualified.
- *The profit margin per sale:* This could, of course, vary. If there are customers yielding a lower level of profit, you may wish to change your sales process to exclude them completely.
- *Customer value and customer retention* (see Chapter 30): How long do your customers remain active? How much will they spend with you over that period? How profitable is their business?
- *The length of your sales cycle:* This is the time between when you generate a lead and when you get paid.
- *The average daily cash balance.*
- *Your aged debtors:* How much you are owed and how quickly your customers are paying you.
- *Your aged creditors:* How much you owe and the length of time it takes you to pay your bills.
- *The value of any stock or inventory you are carrying.*

It Isn't Just About the Money

Building a business is a creative activity. To my mind it is one of the most exciting, interesting and challenging activities it is possible to engage in. Of course, its apparent purpose is to make a profit, but as many entrepreneurs will tell you – especially the accidental ones – it isn't just about money. We are in business because we love it.

ACKNOWLEDGEMENTS

I am most grateful to Ray O'Sullivan and the other founding directors and staff of GreatGas who made it all possible. They are Michelle Gleeson, Maurice Gilbert, Mark Jakeman, Sharon Rankine, Mary Morrissey, Paula Hanafin, Barry Daly, D.J. Cunningham, John Hurley, Seán Kelly and Richard Irvine. The following forecourt owners who decided to join GreatGas and became founding shareholders were also vital:

Paul Connolly, Skibbereen, Cork
Pat and Joe Buckley, Mallow, Cork
Danny, Denis and Anne Cronin, Ballylickey, Cork
Padraig Buckley, Ballybunion, Kerry
Thomas Corrigan, Bagenalstown, Carlow
Jimmy O'Reilly, Aghada, Cork
Jack Kavanagh, Clonroche, Wexford
Tom Liddy, Ennis, Clare
Jack Fitzpatrick, Cahersiveen, Kerry
Pat Lambert, Camolin, Wexford
Con Moloney, Mountrath, Laois
Dermot Murphy, Castletownbere, Cork
Barry and Ger Galvin, Youghal, Cork
John Reilly and John Beirne, Newmarket-on-Fergus, Clare
Daniel, Ronan, Julianne and Ian Cooney, Coachford, Cork

Michael and Doreen Hartnett of COH Transport deserve special mention for their encouragement of GreatGas from the very start, their loyalty to the business and for having the confidence to brand the first GreatGas tanker when we only had a handful of forecourts.

Gerry Wilson, Donal Murphy and Colman O'Keeffe, all of DCC, are acknowledged for their belief in GreatGas. Despite everything, ConocoPhillips also deserve my grateful thanks as without their supply contract, agreed with Paul Barrington, GreatGas would never have gotten off the ground. Louis O'Neill in BDO, Frank Murphy in GMB Solicitors and Michael O'Shea of O'Shea Barry Solicitors provided invaluable corporate finance and legal advice to GreatGas.

I wish to thank my relations – the Murphy, Cunningham, O'Keeffe, Daly and Hickey families – for their ongoing support. I am also grateful to my colleagues in the years since the purchase of GreatGas by DCC. I have in mind Derek and Siobhán Quinlan, Owen and Trish Kelly, Annette Lindsay and especially Sir David Barclay for his advice and encouragement and for writing the foreword to this book.

I am also grateful to the staff of AIB and Ulster Bank for supporting GreatGas to the point where it was able to stand on its own.

GreatGas proudly bears the Churchtown GAA colours on its forecourts all over Ireland as a tribute to the past and present committee and members of a club that has kept the flag flying in Churchtown since 1890.

I do not forget my banking mentors, some of whom I did not recognise adequately at the time; in Bank of Ireland I remember Pat Kennedy, Sean Donelan, Sean McQuaid, Hilary Hough, Ruairí O'Floinn, Adrian Hegarty and Peader McCanna; and in First Active, John Smyth.

My friends, supporters, colleagues and advisers over the years – Bríd Bourke, Gerry Cahill, Gerry Corbett, Pat Cusack, Paul Davis, Gerry Farrissey, Carmel Fox, Dana Hayes, Martin Keaney, Ripton and Rose Kelly, John Lowe, Tom Martin, Simon McAuliffe, Paul McDermott, Steve McGettigan, Sandy Metcalfe, Trish Moran, Donogh Raftery, Tom Shinkwin, Peter Stewart and Derry Walsh – are thanked for their encouragement when it was needed. I also remember Michael O'Driscoll, Margaret O'Brien, Eileen Ahern O'Connor and Peggy O'Flaherty from the Churchtown Village Renewal Trust.

Willy Clingan and Ann Ross, my biking companions for over twenty years, deserve a medal for having to listen to all my plans over the years.

In 2001 I was named Cork Person of the Year for what was described as my 'visionary rural renewal initiative' in Churchtown. It was a great honour to be presented with this award by President Mary McAleese so early in my parish renewal project and I want to thank Brian Crowley MEP, who nominated me, and Manus O'Callaghan, who has selflessly organised these awards for the last 21 years.

And finally, I salute the great people – past and present – of Churchtown in north Cork who have always been my ultimate inspiration, most especially Denis Hickey and the legend that is Noel Linehan.

GM

Index

Index

Index

Index

Ad Sidera
I dTreo na Spéartha
To the Stars[*]

---

[*] These mottos are inscribed on the Millennium Obelisk at Bruhenny Village Green in Churchtown.